Y0-BDI-787

Disney's
WONDERFUL WORLD OF KNOWLEDGE
YEAR BOOK 1990

Wonderful World of Knowledge

GROLIER ENTERPRISES, INC.
Danbury, Connecticut

FERN L. MAMBERG	*Executive Editor*
MICHÈLE A. MCLEAN	*Art Director*
MARILYN SMITH	*Production Manager*

ISBN 0-7172-8241-4
The Library of Congress Catalog Card Number: 78-66149

PRINTED IN THE UNITED STATES OF AMERICA

CONTENTS

1989 AT A GLANCE

JANUARY 20. George H. Bush was sworn in as the 41st president of the United States, and J. Danforth (Dan) Quayle was sworn in as the 44th vice-president. In his inaugural address, Bush urged Americans to become more involved in volunteer activities, and he vowed to end the epidemic of drug abuse.

FEBRUARY 15. The Soviet Union withdrew the last of its troops from Afghanistan, under the terms of an international agreement signed in 1988. Soviet forces had occupied the country for more than nine years, supporting the Communist government in its war with rebel groups. At the height of its involvement, the Soviet Union had about 115,000 troops in Afghanistan.

MARCH 18. The space shuttle *Discovery,* carrying a crew of five astronauts, completed a five-day mission. The mission's highlight was the launch of a communications satellite.

MARCH 24. The tanker *Exxon Valdez* struck a reef in Prince William Sound, south of Valdez, Alaska, and began leaking oil. More than 11 million gallons of crude oil spilled into the frigid waters. The oil spread across the Sound onto many of its islands, covering an area larger than the state of Delaware. Thousands of birds, fish, seals, sea otters, and other animals were killed. The spill was the largest in North American history, and the most serious anywhere in the threat it posed to wildlife.

MAY 8. The space shuttle *Atlantis,* carrying a crew of five astronauts, completed a four-day mission. The mission's highlight was the launch of Magellan, a spacecraft designed to orbit Venus and map its surface.

MAY 18. Soviet leader Mikhail S. Gorbachev completed a four-day visit to China. It was the first summit meeting of Soviet and Chinese leaders in 30 years, ending a period of often bitter disputes. In announcing the "normalization of relations," Chinese leader Deng Xiaoping said, "We want to put the past behind us and chart a new course for the future."

JUNE 4. In China, tens of thousands of army troops moved into Beijing, the capital, to crush a student-led movement for increased democracy that had begun in April. Hundreds of people were killed, and thousands were wounded. In the days following the crackdown, thousands of pro-democracy demonstrators were arrested, and a number of them were executed.

JUNE 19. The government of Burma changed the nation's name to the Union of Myanmar. The name of the capital city was changed from Rangoon to Yangon.

AUGUST 13. The space shuttle *Columbia,* carrying a crew of five military astronauts, completed a five-day secret mission. Despite the secrecy surrounding the mission, it was reported that the main objective was the launching of a spy satellite designed to take highly detailed photographs.

SEPTEMBER 16–22. Hurricane Hugo battered several Caribbean islands, then swept across the Carolinas and into Virginia, West Virginia, Ohio, Pennsylvania, and New York. The violent storm killed at least 48 people, left tens of thousands homeless, and caused more than $6 billion in property damage. The islands of Guadeloupe, Montserrat, St. Croix, St. Thomas, and Puerto Rico were devastated. The hardest-hit cities on the United States mainland were Charleston, South Carolina, and Charlotte, North Carolina.

OCTOBER 16. The African elephant was named an endangered species. Largely because of poaching by ivory hunters, the population of elephants decreased from 1.3 million to 625,000 between 1979 and 1989. International trade in ivory was also banned.

OCTOBER 17. An earthquake measuring 7.1 on the Richter scale of ground motion struck northern California. At least 67 people were killed, and damages were estimated at more than $6 billion. The epicenter of the quake was located on the San Andreas Fault in the Santa Cruz Mountains, about 75 miles (120 kilometers) south of San Francisco.

OCTOBER 23. The space shuttle *Atlantis,* carrying a crew of five astronauts, completed a five-day mission. The main objective of the mission was the launching of the Galileo spacecraft, which began a six-year journey to Jupiter.

NOVEMBER 17. President George Bush signed into law a bill raising the minimum wage. A raise of 45 cents an hour to $3.80 would take effect in April, 1990. A second raise, to $4.25 an hour, would take effect in April, 1991. In addition, a training wage of $3.35 an hour was created for workers under 20 years of age.

NOVEMBER 27. The space shuttle *Discovery,* carrying a crew of five astronauts, completed a five-day military mission.

DECEMBER 2–3. U.S. President George Bush and Soviet leader Mikhail Gorbachev met for talks at Malta, an island nation in the Mediterranean Sea. It was their first summit meeting. Private discussions between the two leaders covered a wide range of subjects. They didn't announce any formal agreements or issue a joint statement. But at the end of the meeting, they held the first joint news conference by U.S. and Soviet leaders. And they both pledged to work for the completion of an arms-control agreement by the time of their next summit, set for June, 1990.

DECEMBER 20. In Panama, 26,000 U.S. troops moved against the government of General Manuel Antonio Noriega and took control of the country. The invasion came after Panama had declared war on the United States and an unarmed U.S. serviceman had been killed by Panamanian troops. Noriega, who was wanted on drug charges in the United States, took refuge in the Vatican embassy. A new government, headed by Guillermo Endara, was installed. Endara had been the leading candidate in Panama's May presidential election, which Noriega had nullified. (On January 3, 1990, Noriega surrendered to U.S. authorities in Panama. He was brought to the United States to stand trial.)

COMMUNISM: WINDS OF CHANGE

The Communist governments of the Soviet Union and Eastern Europe have been known since their founding for political repression. Communist leaders have kept a tight grip on power and have ruthlessly put down dissent. But in 1989, reform seemed to be sweeping through the Communist world at a breathless pace. And the historic changes that took place raised hope for an end to the Cold War—the tension between Communist and democratic countries that has colored world events since the end of World War II.

The changes grew out of reforms begun by Soviet leader Mikhail Gorbachev. Gorbachev came to power in 1985, at a time when the Soviet Union was on the verge of an economic crisis. The economic system was run by the government, and it offered little incentive for workers. As a result, housing and consumer goods—even food and basic items like soap—were in short supply.

Gorbachev began to make reforms in several areas. Under a policy called *glasnost* ("openness"), he allowed more debate on government policies. With a policy called *perestroika* ("restructuring"), he tried to reduce government control of the economy and permit more free enterprise. And in March, 1989, the Soviet Union held its freest election ever. For the first time, voters were offered a choice of candidates for an elected legislature.

But other events made it clear that change in the Soviet Union would be a long, slow process. After years of a state-run system, some people resisted the reforms. And there was unrest in some of the Soviet Union's fifteen republics (divisions)—people began to demand more freedom than the government was ready to give.

Meanwhile, Gorbachev made important changes in Soviet policy toward Eastern Europe. The Soviet Union had set up Communist governments in most Eastern European countries at the end of World War II. And they had sent troops into several of these countries since then to keep the Communists in power. But in 1989, Gorbachev stunned the world by saying that the Soviet Union had no right to intervene in Eastern Europe. And, freed from the threat of Soviet force, Eastern European countries made dramatic reforms.

In country after country, people staged huge demonstrations for democracy—and Communist leaders gave in. In a number of countries, the top leaders resigned and borders with the West were opened. In Poland and Czechoslovakia, Communists gave up their leading role and formed coalition governments with opposition groups. Hungary declared itself a multi-party republic instead of a one-party Communist state. In East Germany, the newly opened borders included the infamous Berlin Wall, which had been built through the middle of the city of Berlin to keep East Germans from escaping. And in Rumania, after the government used force to try to stop demonstrations, the country's Communist leader was executed.

Eastern Europeans greeted these changes with celebrations. And people elsewhere watched the events in East Europe excitedly. The tide of reform that swept through the Communist world in 1989 seemed to mark a turning point in world events.

"I'm hiding. Can you find me?" this katydid might very well be asking. Katydids are just one of the many living creatures that play hide and seek in order to survive.

HIDE AND SEEK

Picture yourself in a lush tropical rain forest. Thick foliage surrounds you, and the air is heavy and still. Suddenly a single leaf stirs on a nearby bush. As you watch in amazement, the leaf sprouts wings and flies away!

The "leaf" isn't a leaf at all—it's an insect called a katydid. Katydids are among the many living creatures that take on disguises in order to survive. By looking like something they're not, animals can succeed in fooling predators. But predators also use disguises—to help them sneak up on their prey.

BLENDING IN

By far, the most common natural disguise is a color or pattern that allows an animal to blend in with its surroundings. This is camouflage. If you've ever taken a walk in the woods, you may have been startled by a bird that suddenly took flight almost at your feet. If so, you've seen camouflage at work: You didn't know the bird was there until you were nearly on top of it.

One of the best-camouflaged woodland birds is the American woodcock. Like many ground-nesting birds, the woodcock is brown, with a splotchy, spotted pattern that blends perfectly with the dead leaves of the forest floor. The female woodcock lays her eggs among the leaves and sits perfectly still to incubate them. As long as she doesn't move, it's almost impossible to tell where the leaves end and the woodcock begins.

The American bittern, a small bird that lives in marshes, carries camouflage one step further. The bittern has a pattern of dark stripes running the length of its neck and breast. When the bird senses danger, it quickly freezes in an upright position, with its bill held straight up in the air. The stripes of its body match the lines of the marsh reeds and cattails perfectly, and the bird seems to disappear. The bittern may even sway in the breeze as the cattails do, to make the disguise complete.

The soft brown of a deer's coat and the gray or brown of a squirrel's fur help these animals blend in with the tree trunks and dead leaves of the woodlands where they live. And like many animals, deer and squirrels have lighter fur on their bellies than on their backs. This coloring is called countershading, and it, too, helps the animals blend in: An animal's underside is always in shadow. Thus the underside would appear darker—and stand out—if it were the same color as the animal's back.

Even patterns that seem to stand out boldly can help disguise an animal. On the open plains, the markings of a giraffe look distinctive. But at dawn and dusk, when the giraffe is feeding at the edge of the forest, its strongly patterned coat seems to fade into the surrounding foliage. It's hard for a predator to pick out the shape of the giraffe against the trees.

Of course, predators can make use of the same camouflage techniques. A tiger's stripes and a leopard's spots help these fierce predators stay out of sight as they stalk their prey through the underbrush.

ANIMAL, VEGETABLE, OR MINERAL?

The all-time camouflage champions may be members of the insect world. There are insects that look like leaves, twigs, bark, flowers, and thorns. There's even an insect that looks like stone—the South African toad grasshopper. This little bug has all the markings of quartz, right down to the dark veining and glistening highlights. When it crouches among the rocks, it seems to be just another pebble. This type of disguise is sometimes called mimicry. And insects are masters at it.

As a Central American treehopper crawls along a branch, it looks in shape and color exactly like a thorn. But if danger comes too close, this "thorn" will suddenly hop away. The Kenyan bush cricket, an African insect,

The American bittern has a pattern of dark stripes on its body, and it lives in marshes. The stripes match the lines of the marsh reeds and cattails perfectly, and the bird seems to disappear among the plants.

takes another disguise. Its color matches the lichens that grow on tree trunks, and its shape blends in perfectly. When the cricket wants to hide, it flattens its legs and antennae against the tree bark—and disappears.

Another insect with a good disappearing act is the praying mantis. This insect's disguise serves double duty—it helps keep the mantis from becoming dinner for a sharp-eyed bird, and it helps the insect find prey. A mantis will often sit motionless on a leaf or branch, quietly waiting to dine on another insect that might come along. Most species of mantis are green or brown and blend in with the plants they frequent. But the exotic African praying mantis wears a pink and green pattern that makes it look for all the world like a flower. Even the parts of its body look like petals. This mantis perches among flowers, hoping a nectar-loving insect will mistake it for one of the blooms.

A group of insects called walking sticks are common in the United States. But if you haven't looked closely, you may never have seen one. During the day, the walking stick hangs motionless in a tree or bush, looking identical to a twig. At night, under the cover of darkness, the walking stick moves from its perch for a tasty dinner of leaves.

Many caterpillars also mimic twigs. The larva of the silver king shoemaker, a Caribbean butterfly, goes one step further: It looks like a dry, curled, dead leaf. The caterpillar crawls to the end of a branch and spins a silken thread, from which it hangs and sways in the breeze like a leaf all day. At night, it crawls back into the tree to feed on leaves.

FLYING LEAVES

The most artful disguises belong to the flying insects. The wings of certain moths and butterflies mimic tree bark, moss—even bird droppings. Some wings imitate leaves so perfectly that they even seem to be flecked with drops of dew. The wings of the Malaysian tussock moth look like dead leaves, and they have transparent patches that mimic leaf decay.

Among the cleverest leaf imitators are the many species of katydids that live in the tropical rain forests of South America. Some of these grasshopperlike insects look like new green leaves; others, like dry and papery dead leaves. And some are mottled with green and brown or flecked with light spots that look like fungus.

A katydid's disguise is complete right down to the veins of the leaf and ragged out-

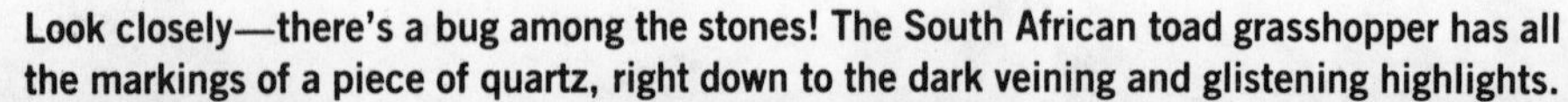

Look closely—there's a bug among the stones! The South African toad grasshopper has all the markings of a piece of quartz, right down to the dark veining and glistening highlights.

The exotic African praying mantis wears a pink and green pattern that makes it resemble the petals of a flower.

lines that look as if sections have been nibbled away by other insects. And katydids seem to know just where to go to blend in. A katydid that mimics the pattern of new green leaves will seek out such leaves and perch among them. A predator may pass within inches of the insect and never know it's there.

WATERY DISGUISES

When it comes to camouflage and mimicry, the creatures of the sea aren't to be outdone by those of the land. The red Irish lord, for example, is a bottom-dwelling fish found along the Pacific coast of North America. Its body is splotched with color—red, brown, white, black. When the fish rests on the ocean floor, it seems to disappear among the algae-covered rocks.

The Sargasso Sea is an area of the Atlantic Ocean that is thick with sargassum weed, a type of seaweed. And here the sargassum fish is right at home. Not only does this fish match the seaweed in color, but its fins have developed into fronds that mimic the leaves of the sargassum weed.

But the ultimate underwater disguise may be that of the glass catfish. The body and fins of this fish are almost as transparent as water—in fact, its internal organs can be clearly seen. The glass catfish spends most of its time hanging motionless in the water. And unless you look closely, it's hard to tell if the fish is there at all.

QUICK-CHANGE ARTISTS

Animals survive by blending in with their backgrounds—but what if the background

It's hard to spot a walking stick until it moves from its perch in a tree: The insect looks identical to a twig.

The glass catfish may have the best underwater disguise. Its body and fins are almost as transparent as water.

changes? A bird that has mottled brown feathers may be well hidden in summer and fall, but when snow falls it will stand out against the new white background.

Many animals change color with the seasons. This is especially so among animals that live in the far north, where the ground is snow-covered all through winter. The snowshoe hare and the weasel wear white coats in winter. In spring, when the snow melts, the animals grow new brown coats for summer.

The ptarmigan, a ground-dwelling bird of the far north, likewise changes color. In spring and again in fall, the bird molts—it sheds its old feathers and sprouts new ones for the coming season.

Some animals can change color much more quickly—and more often—than the ptarmigan. The chameleon is famous for its ability to match its background. When this small lizard is among green leaves, it's green. Put the chameleon on brown earth, and it quickly turns brown.

A number of reptiles and amphibians share this ability to change color. The European tree frog, for example, can alter its skin tone to match the bright green of new leaves or the grayish tone of lichen-covered branches.

Among ocean creatures, the octopus and the flounder are well-known quick-change artists. The flounder is a bottom-dwelling fish, and it changes its color from dark to light depending on the color of the ocean floor. Scientists once tested this ability by placing a flounder in an aquarium with a checkerboard bottom. The fish produced a surprisingly good imitation of the dark and light squares.

How do these animals change color? In all animals, skin color is produced by pigments, chemicals in the skin cells. Animals like the chameleon and the flounder are able to group the pigments in their cells in different ways to produce different shades and colors. A chameleon doesn't really decide to change color—it doesn't think, "Now I'll be green." But its eyes recognize the color around it. The eyes signal the brain, and the brain signals the skin cells to change color.

The crab spider uses pigment in a similar way. The spider crawls into the center of a yellow flower. Then it moves yellow pigment from its intestine to its skin, until it matches the flower perfectly. The spider lies in wait until an unlucky insect comes to sample the flower's nectar—and then it pounces. By taking on a clever disguise, this spider never has to spin a web.

RENTED COSTUMES

An animal that isn't born with a disguise may acquire one. Sloths, for example, are born a grayish brown but gradually take on the color of the trees where they live. Each hair in the sloth's coat is scored with tiny grooves. Over time, algae grow in the grooves, giving the coat a greenish tinge and helping to camouflage the animal.

Spider crabs work much harder at their disguises. As these crabs scuttle around the rocks and coral formations of the ocean, they gather all sorts of materials with their claws—wood chips, bits of coral, tiny sponges, algae, and more. The crab nibbles each find to roughen its edges and then sticks the item onto its shell, which is equipped with tiny bristles. In this way the crab gradually develops a covering that is hard to tell from the ocean floor itself. Its strange habit has earned it the nickname decorator crab.

The flounder is a well-known quick-change artist. It can change its color from dark to light—and even to patterns—depending on the color and texture of the ocean floor.

The io moth has eyes that surprise! The insect's lower wings have markings that resemble two huge, staring eyes. The false eyes are scary enough to startle any bird looking for dinner.

IT PAYS TO ADVERTISE

Not all animals hide to survive. Some take the opposite tack—they advertise, with bright colors and distinctive, eye-catching markings. A saddleback caterpillar, for example, has a bold spot on its back that looks something like a bull's-eye. The caterpillar is also loaded with venom. A bird that bites into one saddleback will remember the taste—and the marking—forever. Thus the marking serves as a warning, protecting saddlebacks from hungry birds.

Such warning markings are common among venomous, bad-tasting, and foul-smelling creatures, from wasps to snakes to skunks. And some animals that taste just fine take advantage of this by mimicking the warning markings of others.

For example, wise birds avoid monarch butterflies. In their caterpillar stage, the monarchs feed on milkweed, which gives them a terrible taste that lasts throughout their lives. Thus a bird that has bitten a monarch quickly learns to recognize these butterflies by their distinctive orange and black markings—and to leave them alone.

Viceroy butterflies, on the other hand, don't have the milkweed taste. A viceroy butterfly would be a fine dinner for a bird. But the markings of the viceroy mimic the markings of the monarch. Since the bird can't tell the difference, it passes the viceroy by.

EYES CAN SURPRISE

The io moth is an insect with a double disguise. When this moth is resting, only its upper wings are visible. Like the wings of many moths, they are colored to match tree bark, helping the io blend in with its surroundings. But if a bird or other predator ventures near enough to discover the moth, the io brings its second disguise into play. It spreads its upper wings to reveal the markings on its lower wings, which resemble two huge, staring eyes. The false eyes are spooky enough to startle any bird, and the bird's hesitation gives the io moth just enough time to flutter safely away.

False eye markings are common among butterflies, moths, caterpillars, and many other creatures. Some, like those of the io moth, are meant to surprise and frighten predators. A swallowtail caterpillar has two large, bulging eyespots on its back. When a bird approaches, the caterpillar puffs up that part of its body, so that it looks like a huge head. The bird is likely to turn away from what appears to be a large, threatening monster.

Other eye markings serve more to confuse predators than to alarm them. Predators often attack their prey around the head and eyes because this is a vulnerable place. Thus the South American false-eyed frog has a set of eye markings on its rump. The frog tucks in its legs and puffs up its body, and a predator doesn't know which end to attack.

The delicate angelfish of the coral reef has a large bold eyespot on its upper fin, all the way back near its tail. A larger fish that is fooled into attacking here will get nothing but a mouthful of tough fin. The angelfish's real eye, meanwhile, is hidden by a dark vertical stripe at its head.

ANOTHER ANGLE

The award for clever deception among ocean creatures has to go to the anglerfish. This fish has a long, flexible spine that protrudes from the tip of its nose. At the end of the spine is a soft, fleshy appendage. The spine serves as a fishing rod, and the fleshy appendage as bait. Depending on the species of anglerfish, the bait may look like algae, worms, or shrimp. In one species the bait looks like a tiny fish, complete with eyes and stripes.

The rest of the anglerfish is colored and patterned to look just like the algae-covered rocks and coral formations where it lives. The angler is nearly invisible as it lies quietly in wait. It dangles its bait out and vibrates it rapidly, to make the bait seem even more lifelike. And when a hungry fish comes along and tries to grab the bait, the would-be eater is promptly eaten by the anglerfish. The angler's clever disguise brings dinner to its door—and helps it survive.

The anglerfish has a long, flexible spine that sticks out from the tip of its nose. At the end of the spine hangs a soft appendage. The spine serves as a fishing rod, and the appendage as bait—to tempt some smaller fish that might be in the neighborhood.

POP GOES THE PAGE!

Open one of these books, and surprise! The pictures slide, jiggle, revolve, and jump right off the page. Pop-up and movable books like these have been around for centuries. Some of the earliest ones date from the 1500's and were used to teach astronomy, with revolving disks and pointers to show the positions of the

Top: In *Creatures of the Desert World,* a newer pop-up book, the plants and animals of the desert come to life. Center: The pop-ups in *Hot Pursuit* show various characters when viewed from different sides—and all the characters are chasing each other. Bottom: Fairy tales, such as the story of Little Red Riding Hood, were popular subjects for movable books of the late 1800's. This scene is from *The Land of Long Ago: A Visit to Fairyland with Humpty Dumpty.*

stars. In the late 1800's, movable books began to be mass produced. They found a new market, as children's books, and fairy tales were a favorite subject. Later, in the 1920's and 1930's, cartoon characters began to pop off the pages. Now, pop-up and movable books are enjoying a revival. Some offer instruction. Some are replicas of earlier books. Some are brand new. But all are designed to be full of surprises!

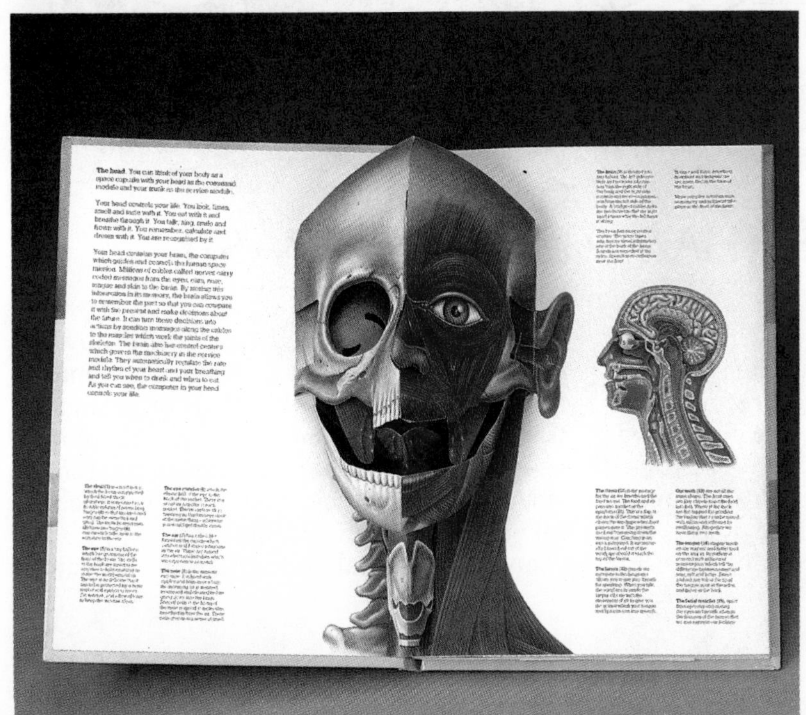

Top: ***Lavinia's Cottage*** **has the charm and flavor of a pop-up book from the late 1800's. Center: The characters from the comic strip** ***Terry and the Pirates*** **stand up in the pages of this book from 1935, a time when cartoon characters were popular in pop-ups. Bottom:** ***The Human Body,*** **published in 1983, has become one of the best-selling pop-up books of all time. Movable illustrations show how the systems of the body work. You can even make a heart beat!**

FLAVOR—MORE THAN JUST GOOD TASTE

Bite into a big red apple, and the flavor explodes in your mouth. Crisp, juicy, sweet and tart at the same time—you recognize it immediately. Without flavor like this, food would be boring indeed.

Everyone has favorite flavors: the sunny flavor of fresh-squeezed orange juice, the rich flavor of chocolate, the salty taste of potato chips, the spicy flavor of a bowl of chili. Flavor has always been extraordinarily important to people. Hundreds of years ago, Christopher Columbus and other explorers sailed across uncharted seas in search of spices to season their food. Today the search for flavor continues—but the setting has changed to the laboratory, where scientists are constantly seeking new ways to imitate and even improve the delicious flavors of food.

TASTE AND FLAVOR

Your enjoyment of an apple or a chocolate bar depends on many factors. Taste—the flavor information provided by your mouth—is only the beginning. What we think of as flavor also comes from a food's aroma, texture, and even temperature.

Many researchers think that people are capable of distinguishing only four basic tastes: sweet, sour, salty, and bitter. These sensations begin as reactions to the chemical makeup of food. Molecules of sweet substances, such as sugar, are different from molecules of salt. And molecules of both sugar and salt are different from those of sour substances (such as the citric acid found in lemons) and bitter substances (such as coffee).

Suppose that you put a piece of candy in your mouth. Saliva immediately begins to dissolve the candy, and sugar molecules are set free. They bathe the taste buds that are located in your tongue, elsewhere in your mouth, and in the upper part of your throat. Each taste bud contains from forty to sixty receptors—special nerve cells that react to the four basic tastes. When a sugar molecule comes in contact with a taste receptor, the receptor instantly fires off a signal to the brain.

The signal travels along one of three major nerve pathways (serving the front of the tongue, the back of the tongue, and the rest of the mouth and throat). At the brain, it is routed in two directions: To the cerebral cortex, which is the main problem-solving area of the brain, and to the hypothalamus and other areas that are involved in the body's perception of pleasure. Thus you identify the sweet taste of the candy and at the same time react with pleasure to it.

But this is only part of the story. If you've ever had a head cold, you probably noticed how flat and boring your food tasted. That's because your nasal passages were blocked—and with them, most of your perception of a food's full flavor.

Odor molecules given off by food rise to your nose as you lift the food to your mouth. Or they may enter the nose through the back of the mouth, where the nasal passages connect with the throat. The odor molecules stimulate nerve cells that, like the taste receptors in your mouth, fire off signals to the brain. But the sense of smell is far more discriminating than the sense of taste—it can distinguish thousands of different aromas. It's aroma, for example, that allows you to tell the difference between chocolate ice cream and vanilla ice cream.

Texture and temperature are important too. There's a big difference in the flavor of cold milk and warm milk. And pudding seems to have a different flavor when it's lumpy. The brain combines the information it receives from the nose and the taste buds with information about texture and temperature, and this makes the identification of the flavor complete.

FLAVORFUL FACTS

Scientists used to think that the four basic tastes were perceived in separate areas of the tongue—sweet at the tip, salty at the sides, and so on. They now know that this isn't true—each taste bud is capable of sensing all four tastes but reacts differently to each one.

Taste may be more acute in one part of the tongue than in another, however. And the sense of taste can vary a great deal from one person to another. Some people have as many as ten times more taste buds than other people—and thus they have a more acute sense of taste.

Children generally like the same flavors their parents like. They tend to favor the foods they grew up with and to distrust new ones.

Scientists called flavorists create artificial flavors in the lab. They take samples of a food and try to "capture" its aroma. Then they analyze the chemical compounds that produce the food's distinctive flavor.

Research has turned up some other interesting facts about taste and flavor. For example, it's unlikely that you'll ever lose your sense of taste. The body is constantly replacing the receptors in the taste buds. In fact, the average receptor is in use only ten or eleven days before a new one develops to take its place. (This ability for regrowth, or regeneration, is very rare for nerve cells.)

Thus, unlike sight or hearing, the sense of taste stays sharp well into old age. Older people sometimes say that their food doesn't taste as good as it used to, but this is rarely because the sense of taste has grown less acute. Instead, the other senses involved in the full experience of flavor—especially the sense of smell—may not be as strong as they once were.

Just as the ability to recognize the four basic tastes lasts throughout life, it seems to be present at birth. And so are certain taste preferences. Newborn babies like sweetness and dislike bitterness immediately. Most people also naturally like salty tastes.

There are sound reasons for these likes and dislikes, scientists say. Sweet foods generally contain sugars that the body can use to produce energy, and salt is essential for many body functions. But many poisonous plants taste bitter. Thousands of years ago, when people gathered their food from the wild, a natural love of salt and sugar and a natural distaste for bitterness helped them survive.

While certain taste preferences seem to be inborn, flavor preferences are much more subject to whim. As a rule, people tend to like flavors they grew up with and to distrust new ones. For example, dishes seasoned with hot peppers and other spices are popular in Latin America and some other regions. Very young children avoid them, but at the age of about 5 or 6 they start to mimic their parents and enjoy these spicy foods. But in many northern countries, hot, spicy foods are considered exotic even by adults.

There are other examples of favorite regional flavors. In Mexico, for example, people enjoy soft drinks flavored with a fruity blend called Jamaica; but this flavor is unknown in many other countries.

Still, flavors such as orange and chocolate are popular all over the world. And while people tend to stay with flavors that they know, there are fashions in flavors. Peach flavor, for example, suddenly increased in popularity a few years ago. Now many food manufacturers say that the trend is toward spicier and more robust flavors.

FLAVOR IN THE LAB

Changes in flavor fashions keep food manufacturers and marketers busy, as they try to stay on top of the latest trends. There's even a special branch of chemistry that's concerned with the study of flavor—and with the creation of flavors in the laboratory. Scientists called flavorists sometimes create flavors that are unlike anything in nature (cola is one such flavor). But more often, they try to duplicate the natural flavors of foods.

To do this, the scientists first take samples of a food and of the aromas it produces. Then they analyze the chemical compounds that produce its flavor and try to decide which ones are essential. Coffee, for example, contains more than 800 different compounds, but not all of them are needed to produce the flavor of coffee.

Often the goal of this research is to reproduce the flavor of a rare and costly substance. Vanilla, for instance, comes from the dried seed pods of the vanilla orchid, which grows only in a few tropical areas. Thus natural vanilla is very expensive.

But there's another reason to find substitutes for some flavors: health. Studies have shown that people today eat far more sugar, salt, and fat than is good for them. Too much sugar and fat can lead to obesity, and fat and salt can contribute to heart disease and other medical problems. Yet sugar and salt are basic tastes that people crave. And fat acts as a flavor enhancer, intensifying the natural taste of many foods. People often find food bland and unappealing when sugar, salt, and fat are taken out—and so scientists want to find good stand-ins for these substances.

So far, researchers have had mixed success with artificial flavors. Some of these flavors are hard to tell from the real ones. But good substitutes for some popular flavors—strawberry and chocolate, for example—have proved harder to create. A good salt substitute also remains to be found. And as researchers have worked to create artificial flavors, people have become more concerned about putting chemicals (including artificial flavors) in their food.

Thus scientists are also seeking ways to boost natural flavors. Through plant breeding and genetic engineering, they hope to produce fruits and vegetables with more concentrated flavors. And in some experiments, they are trying to get tissue cultures (cells taken from plants and grown in the lab) to produce vanilla, cherry, chocolate, and other favorites. If they succeed, you may one day enjoy all the goodness of a fresh-squeezed orange—in a juice that comes straight from the lab.

FIFTY YEARS OF TELEVISION

On April 30, 1939, a small gray screen flickered to life in front of a crowd of onlookers at the New York World's Fair. The age of commercial television had begun.

The signals for that first public broadcast reached only the New York City area, where fewer than 200 television sets were available to receive them. The lucky few who gathered in front of those sets watched in amazement as President Franklin Delano Roosevelt opened the Fair with the statement that "the eyes of the United States are fixed on the future."

Roosevelt couldn't have known what an important part television would play in that future—or how deeply it would affect modern life. Today there are more than 750 million television sets. In North America, television is the most popular form of entertainment and the main source of news. In the average American household, the TV is on for about 49 hours a week—more time than most people spend at work.

In 1989, the television industry celebrated the 50th anniversary of that first broadcast from the World's Fair. It was a time for people to look back over the important developments of the past—and ahead to what may lie in television's future.

TV'S EARLY DAYS

Although U.S. broadcasters chose the opening of the 1939 World's Fair for the formal introduction of commercial television, the technology that made those first daily broadcasts possible had been under development for many years. In the early 1930's, experimental television broadcasts were beamed from the top of the Empire State Building in New York City. Britain began regular television broadcasts in 1936.

When daily broadcasts began in the United States, however, television wasn't an instant popular success. Many people considered it a gimmick—radio with pictures. Only a handful of stations were sending out television signals, and the signals didn't travel very far. Thus people in many areas couldn't receive television. And most of those who could receive the signals were put off by the price of a television set—$200 to $600. This was high enough by the standards of the day to make television a luxury.

Early television sets were nothing like the

large-screen color sets of today. The working parts were housed in bulky wooden cabinets that were meant to look like fine furniture. Fuzzy gray images appeared on screens that were just 5 to 12 inches (13 to 30 centimeters) high. Still, television was intriguing. In the first few years, broadcasters presented live coverage of a wide range of events and programs, from baseball games and cooking lessons to opera and political conventions. World War II put a stop to television broadcasting for several years. But as the war came to an end in 1945, television began to take off.

By 1949, a million television sets were in use in the United States. And by 1959, the number was about 50 million—and growing. Meanwhile, regular service had begun in Canada in 1952.

THE GOLDEN AGE

By the mid-1950's, television was reaching 90 percent of the United States. Programs covered a wide range—broadcasters, it seemed, were unsure what television could do or what the public might want to see, so they tried a little bit of everything.

The first real hit came in 1948 with the start of *Texaco Star Theater*, a variety show that starred comedian Milton Berle. The show was so popular that sales of television sets boomed. Other variety shows soon followed, including *Your Show of Shows*, with comedian Sid Caesar; *The Red Skelton*

Hit shows from the Golden Age of television: *I Love Lucy*, *The Honeymooners*, and *Perry Mason*.

Gunsmoke **was television's longest-running Western. It ran for twenty years, from 1955 to 1975.**

Show; and *Toast of the Town*, which later became *The Ed Sullivan Show*. Like most early television shows, these programs were broadcast live. Whatever happened in front of the TV cameras—planned or unplanned, flubbed lines or brilliant improvisations—was seen on home television screens.

One of the first programs to be filmed rather than presented live was also one of the most popular shows of all time: *I Love Lucy*, starring Lucille Ball. The show, which first appeared in 1951, followed the comic adventures of Lucy and Ricky Ricardo (played by Lucille Ball's real-life husband, Desi Arnaz). The great advantage of recording the show on motion-picture film was that it could be edited before it was broadcast. The film could also be saved—episodes of *I Love Lucy* are still shown in more than 80 countries. (Lucille Ball continued to appear in this and other television series until 1974.)

I Love Lucy helped popularize a new type of show, the situation comedy, or sitcom, which follows the antics of the same group of characters in a new situation each week. Another famous situation comedy from television's early years was *The Honeymooners*, which featured comedian Jackie Gleason as a bus driver who bickered constantly with his wife (Audrey Meadows) and best friend (Art Carney). Many 1950's sitcoms, including *Father Knows Best*, *The Adventures of Ozzie and Harriet*, and *Leave It to Beaver*, presented an idealized picture of family life in the suburbs. Early shows such as *The Goldbergs* and *Amos 'n' Andy* added ethnic flavor to basic sitcom plots.

Television held great appeal for children, and broadcasters were quick to realize this. The first children's show, *The Small Fry Club*, was aired in 1947. It was quickly followed by what became one of the most famous children's shows of all time: *Howdy Doody*. And when *The Mickey Mouse Club* appeared in 1955, mouse-ear caps suddenly became a fad.

Older children enjoyed adventure shows such as *Lassie* and science-fiction dramas such as *Captain Video* and *Superman*. There were also plenty of dramas for adults—spooky tales on *The Twilight Zone*; daytime serial dramas, or soap operas; and crime and detective shows, such as *Dragnet* and *Perry Mason*.

Above all, there were Westerns. *Hopalong Cassidy* galloped onto the screen first, followed by *The Lone Ranger*, *Roy Rogers*, *The Cisco Kid*, and more. By the late 1950's, seven out of the top ten television shows were Westerns. The longest running of all was *Gunsmoke*, which was on the air from 1955 to 1975.

While television entertained millions of viewers with shows like these, it also made them witnesses to important events. Newscasters such as Edward R. Murrow, Walter Cronkite, Chet Huntley, and David Brinkley gained fame for their televised reports. Television provided on-the-spot coverage of the 1952 presidential election.

Of course, television had its share of pure fluff right from the beginning. Game shows such as *Beat the Clock* relied on stunts and pranks for laughs. And a national scandal resulted when it was revealed in 1959 that contestants on some television quiz shows had been given answers so that they could win.

But television's early days also saw some exceptional programs. *Playhouse 90* presented high-quality dramas. *Omnibus* featured live performances and readings by famous musicians and authors. *Amahl and the Night Visitors* was presented in 1951 as the first made-for-television opera, and it became a Christmas classic. Mary Martin flew across the screen in a televised version of the Broadway musical *Peter Pan* in 1955.

Because of the high-quality of these and other early programs, the late 1940's and early 1950's are sometimes called the Golden Age of television. It was a time when broadcasters and performers alike were willing to take chances and experiment on the air.

Star Trek won its widest popularity after it was canceled and appeared as reruns. It's now shown in 80 nations.

NEW SHOWS, NEW CONCERNS

Each decade since the 1950's has had its hit television shows—some acclaimed by critics, some adored by audiences regardless of what the critics said. Most of the types of shows that first appeared in the 1950's are still strongly represented, but they have changed with the times.

Beginning in the 1970's, broadcasters introduced shows that presented women and minorities in less stereotyped ways. Mary Tyler Moore, who had appeared as a suburban housewife in *The Dick Van Dyke Show* in the early 1960's, starred in her own series in the role of a single career woman. The show was an enormous hit. *Julia*, first broadcast in 1968, was the first show to star a black in a role other than that of a servant. (The star was Diahann Carroll, and she played a nurse.) It began a trend in which blacks and other minorities emerged as stars in all types of television shows.

Successful sitcoms of the seventies: *The Mary Tyler Moore Show* (above) and *All in the Family* (below).

Television reflected the social concerns of the 1960's and 1970's in other ways, too. Starting with *All in the Family* in 1971, sitcoms began to take a sharper look at prejudice and other human weaknesses. The next year, *M*A*S*H* took the antiwar sentiment that had built up during the Vietnam War and turned it into a comedy hit.

These trends continued through the 1980's with popular series such as *The Cosby Show* and *Family Ties*. Broadcasters also tried to appeal to young adults with shows such as *thirtysomething* and *L.A. Law*. And soap operas moved into the evening hours with *Dallas*, *Dynasty*, and other popular serials.

M*A*S*H **took the antiwar sentiment of the Vietnam War years and turned it into a comedy hit.**

Sesame Street **is one of public TV's most popular shows. Its imaginative format teaches reading and math skills.**

As host of *The Tonight Show,* Johnny Carson brought wide popularity to late-night talk shows. Quiz and game shows such as *Jeopardy* and *Wheel of Fortune* also continued to be popular. Nostalgia has been in fashion, too, with shows such as *Happy Days* (looking back to the 1950's) and *The Wonder Years* (looking back to the 1960's). And reruns of canceled shows, such as the science-fiction series *Star Trek,* have kept television's past alive.

Westerns, meanwhile, have all but disappeared. They were edged out by other action shows—first by spy dramas and then by crime and detective shows. In keeping with other television trends, some of the new detectives have been women (*Murder She Wrote*) and blacks (*Snoops*).

Broadcasters have also developed some new types of programs. They include made-for-television movies and the miniseries—a drama presented in segments over several nights. (One of the most popular television shows of all time was the 1977 miniseries *Roots*, a dramatization of author Alex Haley's search for his ancestry.) With *60 Minutes* and similar shows, television news developed the "magazine" format—a show divided into segments on different topics, like the articles in a magazine.

Beginning in the 1960's, much quality programming has been presented on public television, which is supported by grants and donations rather than by advertising. Among the most popular public television shows is *Sesame Street,* which uses lively skits, puppets, and animation to teach basic reading and math skills to young children.

Along with changes in programming have come changes in technology. Videotape, introduced in the 1950's, could be edited far more quickly (and cheaply) than motion-picture film. Color broadcasting also began in the 1950's, although it didn't really catch on until the 1960's. (The hit Western *Bonanza,* the first show of its kind to be broadcast entirely in color, did much to popularize color television.)

Television sets changed, too, Transistors and integrated circuits replaced bulky vacuum tubes, allowing manufacturers to make ever smaller portable sets. But manufacturers also made bigger sets—with screens up to 35 inches (89 centimeters) across.

New technology has allowed television crews to travel almost anywhere to cover news and sports events. Millions of people watched the funeral of President John F. Kennedy in 1963, the first steps of astronauts on the moon in 1969, the hearings that led to the resignation of President Richard Nixon in 1974, and the tragic explosion of the space shuttle *Challenger* in 1986.

Television coverage of civil-rights demonstrations in the 1950's and 1960's helped turn the struggle against segregation into a national movement. Later, television coverage of the Vietnam War brought the horrors of combat into living rooms around the world and helped turn public opinion against the war.

Television also captured the attention of millions of people for lighter events. When the Beatles appeared on *The Ed Sullivan Show* in 1964, New York City police noted that not a single crime was committed in the city. Presumably, all the would-be criminals were glued to their television sets.

Because television can have such a strong effect on so many people, it has often been the subject of debate. Nevertheless, television's influence isn't likely to lessen in the future. Television has come a long way since those blurry gray images flickered to life at the 1939 World's Fair, and it's clearly here to stay.

The successful game show *Jeopardy* gives contestants the answers—they have to come up with the right questions.

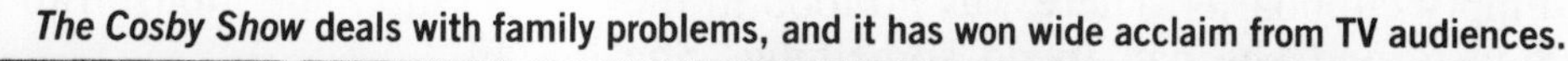
The Cosby Show deals with family problems, and it has won wide acclaim from TV audiences.

A Meal Fit for a Cat

In a warehouse across the street from the Fat Cat Food Factory, Amelia Mouse paced back and forth in her kitchen, staring at her empty cupboards. There was no food in the house, and she had to do something. She couldn't just stand around and watch her children go hungry.

Amelia marched to the front door and stuck her head out. There it was—a fat chunk of cheese mounted atop the meanest mousetrap she had ever seen. And there, too, was Fat Cat, just waiting for her to come out. But Amelia's mind was made up. She was going to get that cheese!

Amelia called her children into the room and gave each of them a hug. "I have to go out," she said. "If anything happens to me, run and get the Rescue Rangers. Do you understand?"

The children nodded and kissed her goodbye. Then Amelia took a deep breath and scurried out the door. She didn't get very far.

Snap! The mousetrap closed on Amelia's tail.

"Well, well," said Fat Cat, licking his lips, "what have we here, hmm?"

Fat Cat carried Amelia to his office. While his back was turned, the children sneaked out and ran for help.

Soon, at Rescue Rangers Headquarters, Chip heard frantic squeaking coming from outside. He went to the door.

At the foot of a nearby tree were four young mice, crying and squeaking.

"Calm down!" said Chip. "One of you tell me what's going on!"

Dale joined Chip, and they listened while the oldest mouse explained.

"Fat Cat took over the factory where we

live, and it's not safe to go out looking for food anymore. But Mama went out anyway, and now Fat Cat's got her!'' A tear slid down the young mouse's cheek, but he quickly wiped it away.

''Don't worry,'' Chip told him. ''We'll save your mother!''

''Come on!'' said Chip, pulling Dale into the house. When they came out again, they were disguised as mice.

They left the children with Gadget, picked up Monterey Jack, and raced to the factory. The three Rescue Rangers crept inside and looked around. The light was dim, but Dale thought he saw some movement along the back wall.

''There he is!'' shouted Dale, excitedly. Chip spun around and clamped a hand over Dale's mouth.

''Quiet!'' he hissed.

Fat Cat was seated at his dinner table. His henchmen, Mepps and Wart, were clearing away the dirty dishes.

''I think I'll have Chocolate Mouse for dessert,'' said Fat Cat, laughing.

Monterey gulped. As he looked around for Amelia, he noticed several vats against the wall marked ''milk chocolate.'' Now he knew what kind of factory they were in.

''We'd better find Amelia before she's dipped, mates!'' said Monterey.

They stayed in the shadows, walking on tip-toe until they spotted Amelia in the corner, shivering with fear, her tail still pinned in the trap.

''All right, men,'' said Chip, facing them. ''I'll distract Fat Cat and the others while you free Amelia.''

Chip scurried across the floor like a mouse, squeaking noisily.

''What was that?'' asked Fat Cat, peering over the edge of the table.

Meanwhile, Dale and Monterey rushed to the trap, lifted the clamp and freed Amelia.

''Thank goodness!'' said Amelia.

''Hurry!'' said Dale, panting. He was using all his strength to keep the clamp from slamming back down and making a racket. Monterey caught the clamp just as it slipped from Dale's grasp, and eased it down noiselessly. Dale looked up and saw that Amelia had reached the door safely.

''Okay,'' said Dale. ''Let's get out of here!''

But Monterey stood frozen in place. His eyes glazed over as the delicious smell of cheese tickled his nose.

''Cheese!'' cried Monterey.

Fat Cat turned toward the familiar voice.

"Uh-oh," said Chip from underneath the table.

"You!" growled Fat Cat, seeing Monterey Jack. "The rest of those pesky Rescue Rangers must be around here somewhere. Get them, boys!"

Dale ran back and smacked Monterey. "Snap out of it!" he urged.

Monterey shook himself. "Huh? Oh! Guess we'd better run for it, matey!"

Wart and Mepps were just about to pounce on them when Dale and Monterey took off in panic. Chip left his hiding place and joined them, and the three rushed for the street.

"Don't let them get away!" yelled Fat Cat.

Wart, Mepps, and Fat Cat bounded after the Rangers. Chip and Monterey made it to the door. But Dale was bringing up the rear and Fat Cat's paw slammed down on his tail.

"Going somewhere?" asked Fat Cat.

Chip and Monterey were out the door before they noticed that Dale was missing.

"Oh, no!" said Chip, looking back. He knew Dale was trapped.

Meanwhile, thinking the Rangers were right behind her, Amelia found her way to Gadget's workshop. But when she arrived alone, Gadget began to worry. She knew something had gone wrong. "I must do something," she said.

Telling Amelia to stay at the workshop, Gadget grabbed her harpoon gun and a quiver of darts, snapped on her tool belt, and jumped into the Rangermobile. When she pulled up to the factory, Chip and Monterey were trying to figure out how to rescue Dale.

"Gadget!" cried Chip. "It sure is good to see you!"

"What happened?" asked Gadget. Monterey explained the situation. Then the three put their heads together and came up with a plan.

"Okay," said Chip, finally. "Let's go."

Gadget gave Monterey the harpoon gun and slipped inside. She hid behind a stack of boxes, then reached for her tool belt and unclipped an old postage stamp. She rolled it into the shape of a funnel and held it to her mouth like a bullhorn.

"Hey, Big Boy," said Gadget purring in Fat Cat's direction. "Over here!"

Fat Cat looked around, trying to locate the voice. Meanwhile, Chip and Monterey made their way across the floor unnoticed.

Wart was dangling Dale over a vat of hot chocolate. Dale covered his eyes, afraid to look down. Monterey aimed the harpoon

gun directly at Wart. "Wait!" whispered Chip. But Monterey had already sent the dart flying. The dart hit Wart's arm.

"Ow!" he cried, loosening his grip on Dale. Dale felt himself slipping out of Wart's fist and screamed.

At that moment, Gadget left her hiding place and headed straight for the vat. Just as she'd hoped, Fat Cat took off after her.

Monterey sent a second dart flying and hit Wart's hand. Wart dropped Dale just as Fat Cat crashed into the vat, knocking it over. Dale landed on Fat Cat's back and slid to the floor.

Gadget tossed the quiver of darts to Chip and Monterey, and they fought off Fat Cat and his gang for as long as they could. Meanwhile, Gadget ran to the door and meowed at the top of her lungs.

Dale ran to the Rangermobile and got it revved up. "Come on!" said Dale. "What's taking so long?"

As Chip and Monterey let the last dart fly, they all heard the one sweet sound they had been waiting for—dogs barking.

"Quick!" called Dale from behind the wheel. "Let's get out of here!"

Chip and Monterey raced outside, and all four took off in the Rangermobile. They rounded the corner just as a pack of dogs tore into the factory. As they rode away, they could hear Fat Cat and his gang screeching and scrambling to find a way out through the back.

Amelia and her children were waiting anxiously back at Ranger Headquarters.

"You shouldn't have any more problems with Fat Cat," Chip told her.

"I don't think he'll go back to *that* factory again," added Dale.

Amelia and the children thanked the Rangers and said good-bye.

That night, Chip made a pot of hot chocolate. "Want some?" he asked Dale, offering him a cup.

"No, thanks!" said Dale, shaking his head. "If I never get close to anything chocolate again in my life, it'll be too soon!"

SPIRALS: TWISTS OF NATURE

The swirling spiral is one of the most beautiful forms in nature—and one of the most common. From tiny one-celled creatures through higher mammals, plants and animals of all kinds seem to favor this pattern above all others. The seeds of the sunflower (above) are packed in a double spiral—one spiral spinning off to the right, and the other to the left. The scales of pine cones grow in similar spiraling patterns. And drops of dew reveal that the true form of a spider's web (below) is a delicate, gossamer spiral, draped between the supporting branches of a tree.

A spiral shape can serve a practical purpose for an animal. When a male Dall sheep (above) fights another male, for example, its horns are powerful weapons. But the spiral of the horns also makes them an excellent helmet, protecting the sheep from the shock of battering blows.

In the plant world, spirals are everywhere you turn. The tendrils of vines such as the pumpkin vine (below) uncurl in spiral form. The petals of many flowers are arranged in spirals. And in many plants, even the leaves are set in spiral patterns.

Scientists aren't sure why spirals are so common in nature, but these patterns seem to be all around us. Outside the world of living things, even tropical storms and vast, distant galaxies swirl in spiral shapes. Next time you take a walk, take a close look and see how many spirals you can find.

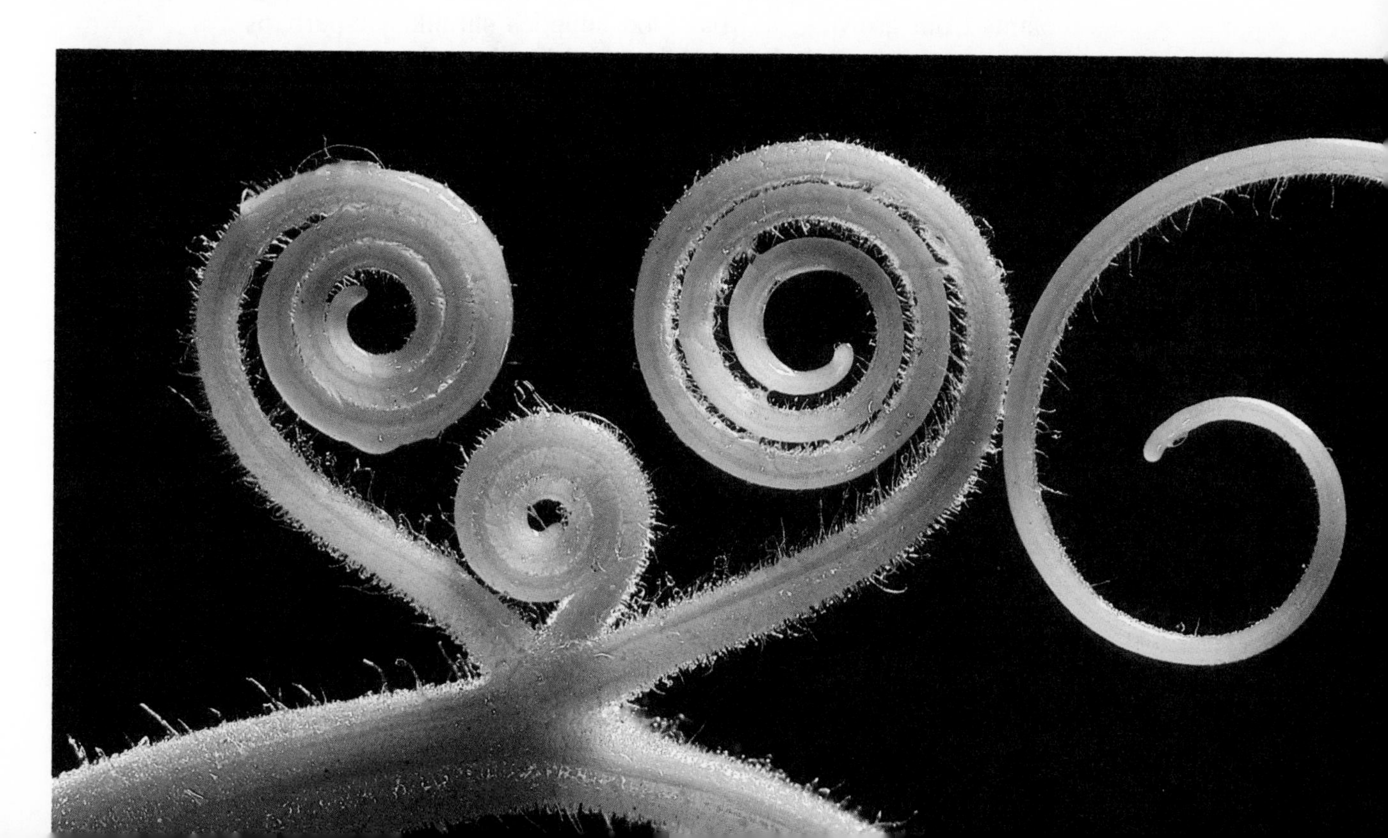

Cutlasstooth

DINOSAURS:
The Way They Might Have Been

Dinosaurs were once the most abundant animals on Earth. But some 65 million years ago, the last of these fabulous reptiles died out. Scientists have proposed many theories for the disappearance of the dinosaurs. Perhaps a giant meteorite struck Earth, sending up clouds of dust that blocked the sun and prevented plants from growing, so that food supplies shrank. Or perhaps other, more gradual changes disrupted Earth's climate, and the dinosaurs simply couldn't adapt to the changing world around them.

Kloon

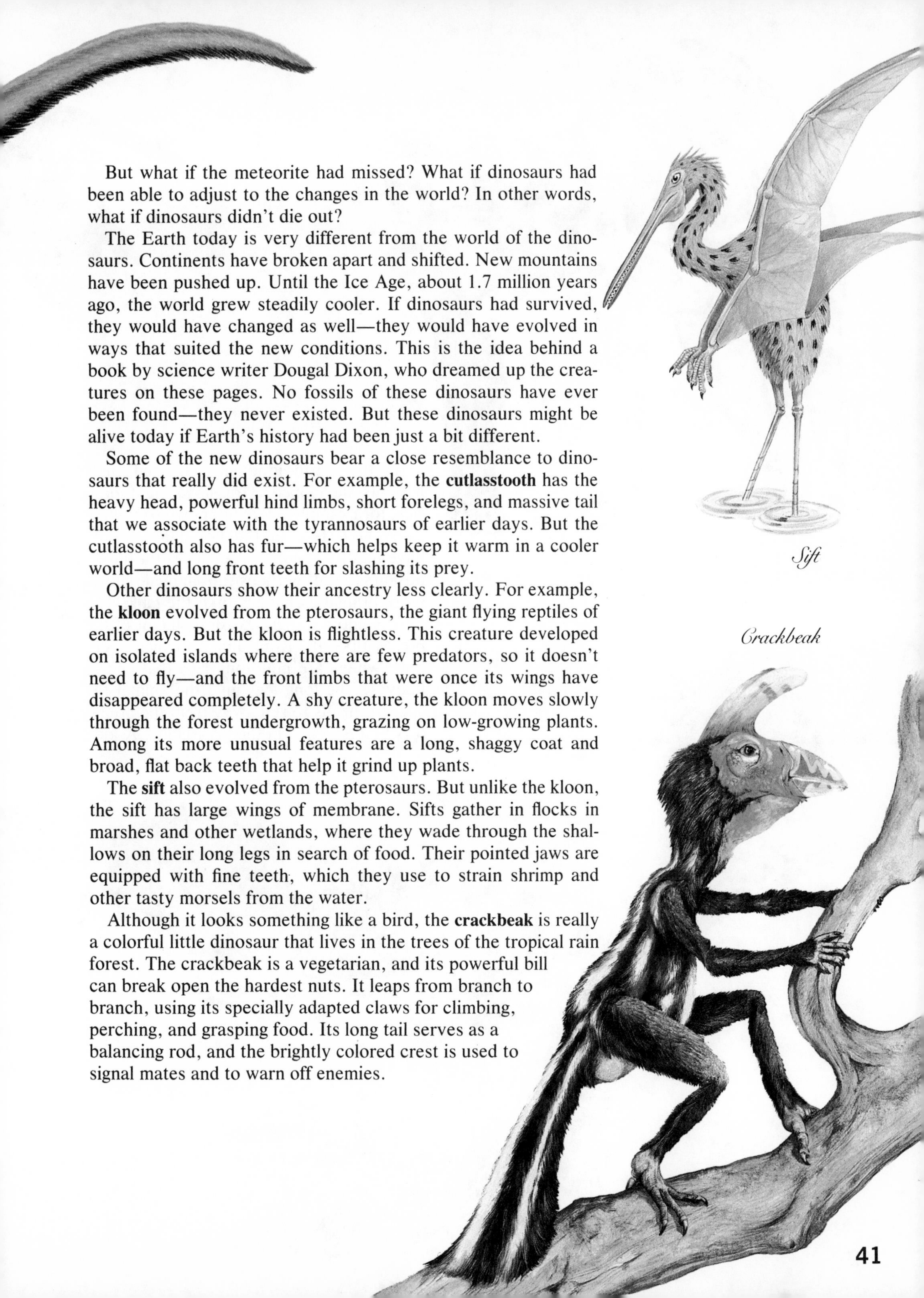

But what if the meteorite had missed? What if dinosaurs had been able to adjust to the changes in the world? In other words, what if dinosaurs didn't die out?

The Earth today is very different from the world of the dinosaurs. Continents have broken apart and shifted. New mountains have been pushed up. Until the Ice Age, about 1.7 million years ago, the world grew steadily cooler. If dinosaurs had survived, they would have changed as well—they would have evolved in ways that suited the new conditions. This is the idea behind a book by science writer Dougal Dixon, who dreamed up the creatures on these pages. No fossils of these dinosaurs have ever been found—they never existed. But these dinosaurs might be alive today if Earth's history had been just a bit different.

Some of the new dinosaurs bear a close resemblance to dinosaurs that really did exist. For example, the **cutlasstooth** has the heavy head, powerful hind limbs, short forelegs, and massive tail that we associate with the tyrannosaurs of earlier days. But the cutlasstooth also has fur—which helps keep it warm in a cooler world—and long front teeth for slashing its prey.

Other dinosaurs show their ancestry less clearly. For example, the **kloon** evolved from the pterosaurs, the giant flying reptiles of earlier days. But the kloon is flightless. This creature developed on isolated islands where there are few predators, so it doesn't need to fly—and the front limbs that were once its wings have disappeared completely. A shy creature, the kloon moves slowly through the forest undergrowth, grazing on low-growing plants. Among its more unusual features are a long, shaggy coat and broad, flat back teeth that help it grind up plants.

The **sift** also evolved from the pterosaurs. But unlike the kloon, the sift has large wings of membrane. Sifts gather in flocks in marshes and other wetlands, where they wade through the shallows on their long legs in search of food. Their pointed jaws are equipped with fine teeth, which they use to strain shrimp and other tasty morsels from the water.

Although it looks something like a bird, the **crackbeak** is really a colorful little dinosaur that lives in the trees of the tropical rain forest. The crackbeak is a vegetarian, and its powerful bill can break open the hardest nuts. It leaps from branch to branch, using its specially adapted claws for climbing, perching, and grasping food. Its long tail serves as a balancing rod, and the brightly colored crest is used to signal mates and to warn off enemies.

Sift

Crackbeak

As the Earth gradually changed, new habitats developed. Grasslands and prairies, for example, were unknown 65 million years ago. Life in the grasslands would have required enormous changes for the dinosaurs. And perhaps no animal shows more dramatic changes than the **lank**. The lank is another flightless descendant of the pterosaurs—its front limbs, which were once wings, are now long legs that end in hooves. The long legs give the animal the speed it needs to run away from the predators that also live in the grasslands. A long

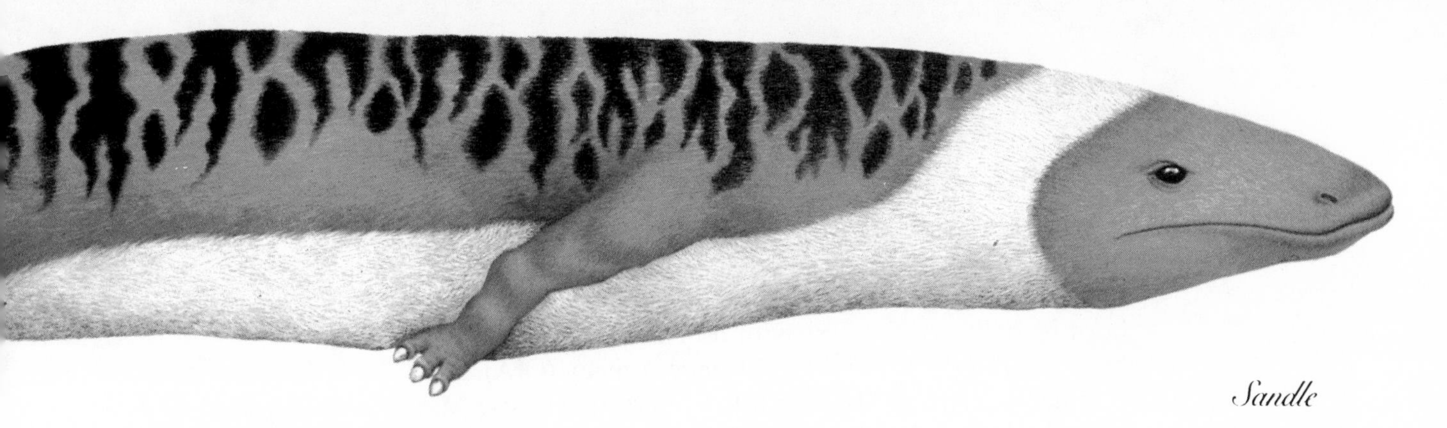

Sandle

neck and snout enable the lank to graze while keeping an eye out for danger, and a coat of mottled fur helps it blend with its surroundings.

The **dwarf megalosaur** is a shoreline predator that evolved in ways suited to the small islands where it lives. It is about 10 feet (3 meters) long—just one third the size of its lumbering, meat-eating ancestors. Small size means that the dwarf megalosaur requires less food, an important factor on islands where food supplies are limited. The dinosaur's size also helps it to be quick and agile. The dwarf megalosaur darts along the island beaches catching seabirds, sometimes even snatching them out of the air.

In other parts of the world, dinosaurs have adapted to all sorts of harsh conditions. The **sandle** is an example. This dinosaur lives in the hot, dry desert, where blistering days are followed by frigid nights. The sandle protects itself from the changes in temperature by burrowing, using its stumpy legs like shovels to dig through the loose desert sand. Once it is buried, only its eyes and nostrils are above the ground—watching and waiting for insects or other small creatures to come along. When this happens, the sandle leaps out and catches its dinner. This predatory dinosaur paralyzes its victims with a poisonous substance in its saliva. And it has adapted to the desert in another way: It never drinks. The sandle obtains all the moisture it needs from the flesh of its prey.

The **mountain leaper** has adapted to the opposite extreme—the cold climate of mountain peaks. A warm-blooded dinosaur, the mountain leaper maintains a constant body temperature even in the snow-capped mountains where it lives. A thick, glossy coat of fur helps. Mountain leapers have also developed unusually large brains, which help them judge distances and make snap decisions as they leap from crag to crag in pursuit of the small birds and mammals that are their prey. These dinosaurs live in packs. The males of the pack do all the hunting, and they also stand guard over the females and the young.

What, you may well wonder, has become of mammals in this dinosaur-dominated world? Very little. While dinosaurs in their many forms continue to rule the Earth, mammals remain lowly little creatures scurrying through the underbrush—just as they were 65 million years ago. Higher mammals, including humans, have never had a chance to develop.

Mountain leapers

PRESIDENTIAL FIRSTS

When George Herbert Walker Bush became the 41st president of the United States on January 20, 1989, he entered history books in many ways. He became the first president to have been born in June . . . the first with four names . . . the first to have been head of the Central Intelligence Agency (CIA).

Other presidents also recorded interesting firsts. Match each "first" in the left column with the appropriate president in the right column.

1. First to have been a professional actor
2. First born in a log cabin
3. Only one elected to a third term (and a fourth)
4. First to be assassinated
5. Only one whose son also became president
6. First to win a Nobel Peace Prize
7. Only one who was both president and vice-president without being elected
8. First sworn in by a woman
9. Only one married in the White House
10. Only one to have served just a month in office
11. First to be born in a hospital
12. First vice-president to become president through the death of a president
13. First to regularly wear trousers instead of knee breeches
14. First one inaugurated in Washington, D.C.
15. Only one who never married
16. First to ride to his inauguration in an automobile
17. Only one to resign
18. First one born in the 20th century
19. Only one to be impeached
20. First whose parents were both alive when he was inaugurated

a. Adams, John
b. Buchanan, James
c. Carter, Jimmy
d. Cleveland, Grover
e. Ford, Gerald
f. Grant, Ulysses
g. Harding, Warren
h. Harrison, William
i. Jackson, Andrew
j. Jefferson, Thomas
k. Johnson, Andrew
l. Johnson, Lyndon
m. Kennedy, John
n. Lincoln, Abraham
o. Madison, James
p. Nixon, Richard
q. Reagan, Ronald
r. Roosevelt, Franklin
s. Roosevelt, Theodore
t. Tyler, John

ANSWERS: 1,q; 2,i; 3,r; 4,n; 5,a; 6,s; 7,e; 8,l; 9,d; 10,h; 11,c; 12,t; 13,o; 14,j; 15,b; 16,g; 17,p; 18,m; 19,k; 20,f.

Next, go on a hunt. The surnames of George Bush and the 20 other presidents listed here (including two Johnsons and two Roosevelts) are hidden in this search-a-word puzzle. Try to find them. Cover the puzzle with a sheet of tracing paper. Read forward, backward, up, down, and diagonally. Draw a neat line through each name as you find it. One name has been shaded in for you.

M	O	H	A	R	R	I	S	O	N	D	O	O	W
N	A	A	J	U	N	O	S	X	E	W	F	O	J
L	F	D	K	E	N	N	E	D	Y	E	S	T	E
O	I	A	I	M	P	N	O	S	N	H	O	J	F
C	M	M	A	S	T	J	A	E	T	T	U	T	F
N	A	S	E	K	O	A	Y	N	J	U	R	N	E
I	H	A	R	D	I	N	G	M	A	B	E	A	R
L	E	W	E	R	U	E	R	I	C	H	F	R	S
H	G	A	L	I	O	Q	O	J	K	E	C	G	O
E	D	R	Y	B	U	O	O	T	S	H	I	U	N
C	I	O	T	A	E	H	S	D	O	O	S	I	B
A	M	S	M	B	N	T	E	E	N	F	X	U	M
R	O	X	K	S	P	O	V	E	V	O	O	U	B
T	R	A	O	A	P	R	E	M	N	E	B	R	I
E	C	N	B	D	N	A	L	E	V	E	L	C	D
R	E	A	G	A	N	S	T	R	E	W	A	T	Y

ZAP!

It's four o'clock on a summer afternoon. But judging from the color of the sky, it might be nearly night. Angry, slate gray clouds are piling up, and a feeling of tension builds in the air. Then—ZAP! A blinding flash zigzags across the sky, followed by a sharp clap of thunder.

Scenes like this take place all around the world millions of times each day. Lightning is one of nature's most spectacular events, but it's also one of the most common. In fact, lightning is so common that we tend to underrate it—its power, its potential for damage, its mystery. Now, however, scientists are giving lightning a closer look, hoping to learn more about it.

OPPOSITES ATTRACT

For centuries, people had no idea what caused lightning. The ancient Greeks and other early people believed that thunder and lightning were created by the gods, perhaps as a way to show their anger. The truth about lightning began to be learned in the 1700's, after electricity was discovered. Today scientists have a fairly good idea of what happens when lightning strikes—although some details still remain unclear.

Lightning is a huge spark of electricity. It can form in snowstorms, sandstorms, tornadoes, the clouds over volcanic eruptions, and nuclear explosions. But it is most common in thunderstorms. Electric charges build up in storm clouds. Areas with positive charges usually develop in the top of the cloud, and areas with negative charges develop near the bottom. Positive and negative charges attract each other. So, when the attraction between the separated charges becomes strong enough, the charges leap toward each other in a rapid electrical discharge, producing lightning.

Lightning can travel inside a cloud, when the positive and negative charges within a cloud create a discharge (this is the most common form of lightning). It can also travel from one cloud to another, when the charge of one cloud attracts the opposite charge of another. This produces the biggest bolts of all—some spanning more than 150 miles (240 kilometers). But most of the lightning that people see is lightning that travels from a cloud to the ground, when a charge from a cloud meets an opposite charge on the ground.

What you see as a single stroke of lightning, however, actually develops in stages. First, a faintly luminous electrical discharge heads toward the ground in a series of jumps, sometimes forking and branching on the way. When this *stepped leader* is still some distance from the ground, it begins to attract electrical discharges called *streamers* from trees, hills, and other points.

The electrical charge carried by the streamers is the opposite of that carried by the leader. The moment a streamer meets the leader, an enormous surge of current—thousands of times stronger than the electrical current in your house—is produced. This surge, called a *return stroke,* causes the air along the path of the leader to glow brilliantly, producing what we see as the lightning flash.

Often the first stroke is followed rapidly by three or four more strokes, traveling up and down the same path. Sometimes there are as many as twenty. The strokes are so quick that we generally see a single bolt of lightning, flickering in the sky. But occasionally the path of the bolt is displaced by the wind, so that repeated strokes follow separate but parallel paths. This is called *ribbon lightning*.

The thunder that follows lightning begins as a shock wave produced by the stroke. The stroke's enormously powerful current heats the air by thousands of degrees, to temperatures that may be five times as hot as the surface of the sun. The intense heat causes the air to expand rapidly, and this rapid expansion creates the shock wave. As the wave travels out from the lightning, it becomes an ordinary sound wave.

Thunder continues to rumble for a while as sound waves from higher and higher along the track of the lightning gradually reach your ears. More than 20 miles (30 kilometers) from a storm, thunder generally can't be heard. But lightning may still be seen. These distant, silent flashes are sometimes called *heat lightning*.

When lightning travels within a cloud, the bolt often can't be seen. Instead, the cloud seems to glow as the flash lights it from within, a spectacle known as *sheet lightning*. Lightning can produce other unusual effects. *Bead lightning* occurs when a long flash ends in a series of glowing beads along the path of the bolt. *St. Elmo's fire* is an eerie, glowing electrical discharge that can be seen around aircraft, towers, and the tall masts of sailing ships.

Stranger still is *ball lightning,* a glowing ball that floats above the ground after a lightning flash. Ball lightning has been said to float right through windows and down chimneys into people's homes. Scientists don't know how or why it forms. In fact, some suspect it's an optical illusion.

However, the proverbial "bolt from the blue"—that is, lightning that strikes unexpectedly out of a clear sky—definitely can occur. Bolts of lightning have struck miles away from the storms that formed them.

ELECTRIFYING RESEARCH

Lightning almost certainly brought fire to early people. Some researchers think it may have started life on Earth, by delivering a charge to the soup of chemicals that made up the planet's early atmosphere. In an experiment, scientists demonstrated how this might have happened. They ran an electrical current through a mixture of gases and discovered that organic molecules—the building blocks of life—formed as a result.

But if lightning has brought benefits, it is also a powerful destructive force. On the average, about 100 people in the United States are killed by lightning each year, more deaths than from any other type of natural disaster. Several hundred more people are struck but not killed. (One park ranger was reportedly hit by lightning seven separate times.) The reason more people aren't killed is that a lightning stroke, while enormously powerful, is very brief. All the same, the force can stop a person's heart and breathing. Quick first aid is often the key in saving lives.

Lightning also destroys and damages thousands of buildings each year. It does millions of dollars worth of damage to electrical equipment by sending surges of power through the lines. It starts fires that destroy vast stretches of forest. And it poses a serious threat to aviation and space research.

This power for destruction is leading scientists to study lightning more closely. They have already learned a great deal. Careful measurements have shown that the return stroke of a lightning flash forms much more quickly, and may be many times more powerful, than had been thought. This means that devices such as surge protectors, which are designed to prevent damage to electrical equipment, may need to be improved.

Meanwhile, some old myths about lightning have been disproved. It's not true, for example, that lightning won't strike the same place twice. It can, and it often does. In fact, because of their land formations and air currents, some places are hot spots for lightning and get far more than their fair share of strikes.

Some research is hoping to build on this knowledge and find ways to predict lightning. By locating areas that are prone to lightning and by monitoring the electrical fields in storm clouds, forecasters may one day be able to issue lightning warnings in the same way they now issue tornado warnings.

Other research is focusing on protection for airplanes and spacecraft. Most airplanes are struck by lightning an average of once a year. Yet no one inside is harmed, and the planes keep flying. This is because the metal shell of the airplane conducts, or carries, the electricity around the outside of the plane—the charge never enters the interior. (Scientists call an arrangement like this a Faraday cage, after the 19th-century British scientist Michael Faraday.)

Planes of the future, however, will probably be made of materials such as graphite and epoxy, which don't conduct electricity as well as metal. But they will also depend more heavily on electronic systems that could be damaged by lightning. Thus they will need greater protection. Adding to the concern is the fact that rockets and many aircraft don't just wait for lightning to strike. Often these craft trigger lightning, by producing an electrical field that acts as a leader and calls forth a return stroke from a storm cloud.

SAFETY FIRST

For the most part, knowledge is still the best protection against lightning. Experts say that you should never underestimate the power and danger of a thunderstorm. When a storm begins to brew, go indoors—ideally, into a building equipped with a good system of lightning rods. These systems consist of metal rods and wires that "catch" the lightning and conduct it safely to the ground, so it doesn't vent its full force on the building.

Even without lightning rods, you'll probably be safe in a large building such as a house. Turn off televisions and other equipment that could be damaged by a power surge. Keep back from doors and windows. Take your bath or shower later—metal pipes and the water in them can carry electricity. So can telephone wires, so stay off the phone.

Another safe spot is inside a car. Like the shell of an airplane, the metal body of the car forms a Faraday cage that carries the electricity around the outside. Roll the windows

A SHOCKING STORY

In 1752, in a now-famous experiment, Benjamin Franklin flew a kite in a thunderstorm. A metal key was attached to the kite string, which Franklin held in his hand. Electricity from the storm clouds traveled down the wet kite string to the key—and he felt the shock. The experiment proved that lightning is a form of electricity. It also proved that Franklin was lucky—he could have been electrocuted. In fact, some people who have tried to repeat his experiment have been killed. So when thunder clouds begin to form, keep your kite inside the house!

up to help complete the cage. (Glass itself won't conduct electricity, but the water running over it in a storm will.)

Stay out of tents and small sheds that stand alone in open areas. These structures are likely targets because lightning tends to strike high points. For the same reason, don't stand under an isolated tree.

If you are caught in the open with no shelter, try to find low ground, such as a gully, and squat down. Most experts say that you shouldn't lie down, however. The ground can conduct electricity; if you stretch out and lightning strikes nearby, you may get more of a shock than you otherwise would. Some people think that wearing rubber-soled shoes will help because rubber is an insulator —that is, it doesn't carry electricity. But it's unlikely that a thin strip of rubber could offer much protection from the force of a lightning bolt.

Be sure to stay away from water and anything else that conducts electricity well—wire fences, metal railings, and the like. And if you're with a group, spread out. You'll be a more likely target for lightning if you are bunched together.

If you follow these safety rules, you'll have nothing to fear from lightning. The next thunderstorm will find you safe and dry inside your house, watching one of nature's most spectacular shows.

Fads: They come in and they go out . . . and sometimes they come in again! Hula-Hoops, Davy Crockett coonskin caps, and "smile" faces—all fads from years ago—were popular once more in 1989.

WHAT'S IN, WHAT'S OUT—AND WHAT'S IT ALL ABOUT?

In a clearing, dancers whoop and gyrate wildly. Each wears an elaborate fur headdress, with a bushy animal tail hanging down behind. As the dancers twist, brightly colored rings spin around their hips.

An exotic tribal rite? No. The "clearing" could be your own backyard; the "dancers," any group of average people. They're just enjoying the rebirth of two popular fads of the 1950's: Hula-Hoops and coonskin caps.

The hats and hoops are silly, of course—but like most fads they're also fun. If you missed seeing these offbeat items in 1989, perhaps you spotted the return of another fad from the past: the "smile" face. In 1970, these grinning faces adorned everything from buttons and balloons to golf balls and coffee cups. In 1989 they popped up again—even on high-fashion clothes.

Every era seems to have its fads—toys, activities, foods, and clothes that come in, suddenly are all the rage, and just as quickly go out again. The 1980's were no exception. Car window signs—"Baby on Board" and dozens of spinoffs—became nearly as

Another fad that seems to have staying power is skateboarding. But telephone-booth stuffing, a silly fad of the Fifties, hasn't been seen in years.

popular as "smile" faces were in 1970. In place of coonskin caps, people wore antenna-like Deely Bobbers.

Children of the Eighties collected stickers of all kinds—and they pined for Cabbage Patch Kids. For a short time, in fact, these dolls were so popular that their manufacturer couldn't make enough of them. Children waited months—and some parents even flew to other countries—to get them. Now you can find the dolls in any toy store, but they're not big sellers. As with most fads, their day has passed.

How do fads like these get started? Some, like Hula-Hoops, are dreamed up by manufacturers. The Hula-Hoop was developed by a toy company that heard of children using bamboo hoops in exercise classes in Australia. The company started making the hoops in bright plastic and promoting them with playground demonstrations.

By mid-1958, Hula-Hoops were all the rage. Kids—and adults—everywhere were twirling them around their hips, legs, and arms, sometimes several at a time. There were Hula-Hoop contests, to see who could keep a hoop spinning for the longest time. By the time the fad died out, more than 50 million of the plastic rings had been sold.

A fad like the Hula-Hoop can bring millions of dollars to a toy manufacturer. Thus manufacturers are always trying to guess

Young children of the Eighties collected Cabbage Patch Kids. Older children made and wore embroidery-thread friendship bracelets.

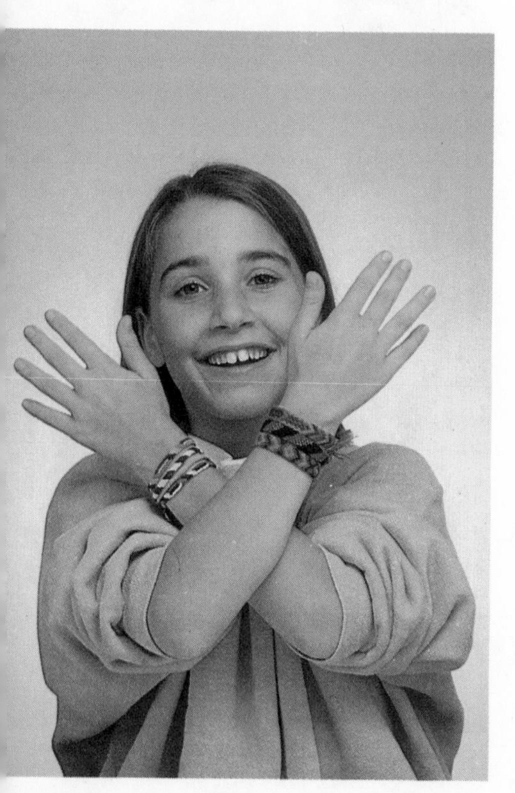

what the next fad will be. Some even hire professional fad forecasters. And there's an annual fad fair, where inventors can show off their latest ideas.

All the same, it's hard to predict which crazy item will catch on next. The "smile" face first appeared in 1962, as a promotional symbol for a New York City radio station. It wasn't until eight years later that it suddenly took the country by storm.

Besides the "smile" face, the 1970's produced one of the most ridiculous fads of all time: the Pet Rock. This item was nothing more than a rock in a box. But for a short time, Pet Rocks sold like . . . well, Hula-Hoops.

Some fads are kicked off by films and television. Coonskin caps are an example. After the adventures of the famous frontiersman Davy Crockett were depicted in a popular film and television series, the caps—modeled on the headgear he wore—popped up everywhere. More recently, the hottest craze was for rainbow-striped suspenders like those worn by the alien Mork in the television series *Mork and Mindy*.

But just as often, fads have little to do with toy makers, television, or anything else you can put your finger on. They just seem to spring up and catch on by themselves. There's no real reason, for example, for the current popularity of embroidery-thread friendship bracelets. Kids everywhere just seem to enjoy making and wearing them.

These spontaneous fads are often some of the silliest of all. Take telephone-booth stuffing, for example. In the late Fifties, a group of bored college students decided to see how many people could squeeze into a phone booth. The stunt spread quickly from

In the Seventies, Pet Rocks were one of the most ridiculous—and one of the most popular—fads of all time.

campus to campus. (The record was 34 people.) And when students tired of squeezing into phone booths, they stuffed themselves into other objects—hollow trees and compact cars.

High school students of the 1940's thought up another strange fad: Friends would exchange one shoe and one sock, and each would walk around with mismatched footgear for a day. In the Thirties, marathon dance contests were in. People danced around the clock for days, weeks, and sometimes months, until they dropped from exhaustion. Some did it for fun. Others, sadly, did it to earn a few dollars—this was the era of the Great Depression, when many people were out of work.

Like fads before and after them, shoe swapping and marathon dancing have come and gone. But occasionally, a fad stays around to become a permanent fixture. The yo-yo, for instance, was introduced in 1929 and quickly became the rage. No one expected it to be around for very long. But, while yo-yos have had their ups and downs, they've never really gone out of style. Today the yo-yo is a classic toy.

Another fad with staying power is the skateboard. Skateboarding started in the 1960's among surfers and a few teens. Now millions of people are doing it—and doing it seriously. There's even talk of making skateboarding an Olympic sport.

Even if skateboards become passé, they may not be gone forever. There's always a chance that a fad will stage a comeback—as Hula-Hoops, coonskin caps, and "smile" faces seem to have done. Why? It's anyone's guess. Nostalgia for the past may have something to do with the return of these items. But the most likely reason is the one that's behind most fads: fun.

BASEBALL MEMORIES

Ah, baseball. Green fields and blue skies on a summer afternoon. The windup and the pitch. The crack of the bat. A tiny white pellet soars far and deep, disappearing into the grandstand. The hometown fans go wild. Hey, get your peanuts! Get your popcorn!

Ah, baseball. That grand old game. Uniforms change, stadiums change, but the game stays the same. Adults recall great players and thrilling moments of the past. Kids memorize statistics and collect baseball cards of today's stars. Every season adds a new chapter to the long and colorful history of "the great American game." And for baseball and its millions of followers, a trio of anniversaries made 1989 an especially historic year.

MILESTONES

America's national pastime turned 150 in 1989, or so legend has it. In 1839, the story goes, baseball was invented by a West Point cadet named Abner Doubleday, in the village of Cooperstown, New York. Doubleday, it is said, made up the basic rules of pitching and hitting, marked out the first diamond-shaped field, and organized a group of boys into two teams.

Most historians no longer credit Doubleday with inventing the game. They say that baseball evolved from the British sport of rounders, and that a New York bank teller named Alexander Cartwright drew up the first rules in 1845. But whatever the true origins of the sport, Cooperstown has long been regarded as the "home of baseball."

On June 12, 1939, to commemorate the game's 100th anniversary, the National Baseball Hall of Fame and Museum was opened in Cooperstown. In addition to honoring the sport's pioneers and greatest players, the facility grew to house a vast collection of baseball memorabilia and to become the game's most fabled institution.

On June 10, 1989, the Hall of Fame celebrated its 50th anniversary with a daylong series of gala events: a parade with the theme "Memories and Dreams"; the dedication of a new wing (to be completed in 1990); the release of a U.S. postage stamp

honoring Lou Gehrig (a 1939 inductee); and an old-timers game featuring former major-league stars.

Meanwhile, fans looked back on 50 years of baseball on television. The first game ever to be televised was aired on May 17, 1939—the second half of a college doubleheader between Princeton and Columbia. The first major-league game to reach the airwaves was an August 26 contest between the Cincinnati Reds and the Brooklyn Dodgers.

The enormous popularity of baseball today owes much to television. In the 50 years since those first fuzzy images flickered across the screen, television has enabled generations of fans to witness many historic moments and to follow their favorite teams all season long.

BASEBALL CARDS—TIES TO THE PAST

They are almost as old as baseball itself, and they are as much a part of its tradition as peanuts and Cracker Jack. Baseball cards are memories—collected, traded, bought and sold, or just stored in a shoe box. Hall of Fame slugger or obscure relief pitcher, every player who has donned a major-league uniform is enshrined on a baseball card. In 1989, baseball cards were more popular than ever. Kids were buying them by the millions, and adult collectors were paying record amounts for old and rare cards.

The first baseball cards were issued in the 1880's and distributed in cigarette packs. Today they come in packages of about fifteen, along with a stick of bubble gum, a puzzle, or another bonus item. There are five major producers—Topps, Donruss, Fleer, Sportflics, and Score—who sell about five billion cards a year.

For many, collecting baseball cards isn't just a hobby. Some dealers pay hundreds or even thousands of dollars for old and rare cards. In recent years, the value of such collectors' items has been skyrocketing. The most valuable card on the market today is said to be the 1909 Honus Wagner, priced at more than $35,000. Generally, rookie cards (first cards) of star players are in great demand. For example, a 1952 Topps Mickey Mantle could sell for about $7,000. So, if you've got any old baseball cards, don't throw them out!

The Loch Mess Monster

Scrooge McDuck made a final check of his scuba gear. ''Ready to go in after the Loch Mess Monster, Uncle Scrooge?'' asked his nephew, Louie, who was helping his two brothers row their small boat to the middle of Loch Mess.

''All ready, boys!'' answered Scrooge. ''Now all we have to do is wait for Messy to show her pretty face.''

''How do you know she will, Uncle Scrooge?'' asked Webby, turning to look at him from the front of the boat.

''The villagers have seen her every sundown at this time for a week,'' replied Scrooge. ''And then one of their sheep disappears. I don't think she'll disappoint us tonight.''

Scrooge rubbed his hands together in anticipation. He smiled as he thought of the money he would make once Messy was captured. Every museum in the world would pay a fortune for a living specimen from the age of the dinosaurs. The villagers might reward him, too, for ridding them of a sheep-stealing monster.

''Now remember the plan, boys,'' said Scrooge. Huey, Dewey, and Louie repeated the steps Scrooge had made them memorize.

''First, Uncle Scrooge dives after Messy and ties this rope to her tail,'' said Louie, holding up a piece of strong rope that was attached to the bow of the boat.

''Then Messy will tow us to her hideout while Uncle Scrooge follows behind,'' Dewey added.

''And once we know where she hides, we'll come back later and capture her,'' finished Huey.

Huey no sooner spoke than the boat began to rock back and forth. The sun was already low on the horizon, and in the fading light, Louie caught sight of a dark shape coming straight for them.

''Get ready, Uncle Scrooge!'' Webby

called. "Something's coming." Scrooge put the breathing tube in his mouth, lowered the mask, and jumped over the side of the boat, holding the rope.

As the dark shape in the water grew larger, the boat began to heave back and forth.

"I see its head!" yelled Dewey.

"Its coming right for us!" yelled Louie. "Everyone hold on tight!"

A gigantic body swept past them and slipped beneath the dark waters of Loch Mess. The rope began to uncoil. The little boat lurched forward and began to bump across the lake like a water skier pulled by a power boat.

"Uncle Scrooge must have roped her!" yelled Louie, but his words were lost in the wind as they streaked across the lake. Suddenly the boat crashed to a halt, and all four ducks landed in a pile in the bow of the boat.

"What a ride!" gasped Huey, sitting up to look around. "I wonder where we are." They peered cautiously over the side of the boat, only to find it resting peacefully on the lake shore.

"Where's Messy?" asked Louie.

"And where's Uncle Scrooge?" asked Webby.

"Oh, he'll be all right," said Dewey. "He'll just swim to shore. I'm more worried about us. It's dark and we don't know where we are."

They decided to stay where they were until morning. While Webby and Huey made camp, Louie and Dewey went to look for firewood.

"Hey! Over here!" shouted Louie. Huey and Webby followed his voice and found him standing near the mouth of a cave, not far away.

After a quick search, they found a lantern and some matches. In minutes, the lantern was flickering brightly, lighting the inside of the cave.

"Wow!" said Huey. "Just look at all this stuff."

There were bicycle pumps, cans of spray paint, and big car inner tubes littering the floor of the cave. But Webby found the biggest surprise.

"Oh, look!" she cried, as she ran over to seven big, beautiful sheep, all tied together. "I bet these are the villagers' missing sheep."

"Something fishy is going on here," said Dewey.

"Yeah," said Louie. "And I don't think

it has anything to do with a sheep-stealing sea monster.''

"You got that right,'' said a familiar voice. They turned in surprise to see four figures standing behind them at the cave entrance, holding a string of inner tubes painted to look like a monster and leading a frightened sheep.

"The Beagle Boys!'' gasped Huey. "Why, you guys have been stealing sheep and using a fake monster to make the villagers think it was Messy.''

"Grab them,'' Big Time ordered. The other three Beagles caught the boys, while Big Time grabbed for Webby. But he missed. In seconds, she had disappeared down a dark tunnel.

"Let her go,'' said Bouncer. "She'll be back. There's no other way out of the cave.''

"You'll never get away with this!'' yelled Louie, as Big Time tied their hands together.

"Who's to stop us?'' he grinned. "While the villagers are looking for a sea monster, we'll be driving their prize sheep to the auction in Invermess. We'll make a bundle on this scheme. All we gotta do is keep you guys out of the picture, so the villagers don't wise up.''

After the boys were securely tied, Bouncer backed a truck into the cave, and Burger and Baggy began loading sheep. But no sooner had they loaded the first one than an eerie sound stopped them in their tracks.

"What was that?'' Baggy whispered, looking toward the tunnel where Webby had disappeared. A second eerie call sent the Beagles out of the cave on the run. All except Big Time. He reached behind a bale of hay and drew out a small, wet figure.

"It's Scrooge McDuck!'' he barked. "What're you doin' here?'' Big Time reached for Scrooge's air tank. "You makin' monster noises with this?'' he laughed.

"Come back, boys,'' he called. "It's only the mysterious monster McDuck.''

The Beagles peered into the cave and, seeing it was only Scrooge, they returned to their work. Big Time tied Scrooge up and left him with his nephews.

As the last sheep went into the truck, a horrible roar sounded from the mouth of the tunnel.

"Quiet down, Scrooge," yelled Big Time. "We won't fall for your trick another time."

Then a giant shadow fell across the truck. "What's that?" asked Baggy. Another roar sounded, and the Beagles looked up to see a real, live sea monster step from the tunnel, with Webby on her back.

"After 'em, Messy!" she ordered. The sea monster took one huge step toward the Beagles.

"Run!" Big Time yelled as he tried to escape. But he was no match for Messy. One flick of her gigantic tail knocked him off his feet. The rest of the Beagles gave up. Webby slid down from Messy's back and freed the boys and Scrooge. Together they tied up the Beagle Boys and loaded them into the truck while Messy stood guard.

Once the Beagle Boys were safely out of the way, Webby said, "Uncle Scrooge, I was so worried about you! What happened after you jumped into the water?"

"I grabbed the rope and Messy pulled me right into an underwater entrance to this cave," he explained. "Then the rope broke and I lost her. I wandered around until I found the boys here and tried to scare the Beagles away."

"But it was Messy who really did the scaring," said Webby. The sea monster put her head down so Webby could pet her.

"Now that she's rescued us, you won't really sell her to a museum, will you, Uncle Scrooge?" asked Webby.

"No! I couldn't do that. I see now that some mysteries are better left unsolved. Messy's secret will be safe with us." Messy leaned over and gave Scrooge a big kiss.

"Phew!" said Scrooge. "She smells like fish."

"Well, what did you expect from a real, live Plesiosaur?" giggled Webby. "They don't really eat sheep, you know."

The floating, clover-shaped leaves of this water fern are just one of many kinds of leaves in nature. Besides producing food, many leaves have special features.

LEAVES UNLIMITED

Flowers are the showoffs of the plant world. They're the part of a plant that catches the eye and the part that people usually think is the most beautiful. Leaves, on the other hand, are often overlooked—just green background for the showier parts of the plant.

But take another look. A plant's leaves may be just as beautiful as its flowers, and sometimes even more so. And the importance of leaves goes far beyond their beauty: Most plants make their food in their leaves. Since all higher forms of life—including people—survive by eating plants (or eating animals that eat plants), it's likely that none of us would be here if it weren't for leaves.

Plants have an enormous range of different leaves, from huge palm fronds to tiny pine needles. In fact, each species of plant has a different type of leaf, and even on the same plant no two leaves will be exactly the same. And while food production is the most important job of leaves, many leaves are designed to play almost unlimited roles.

FOOD FACTORIES

The process by which leaves make food is called photosynthesis. This term comes from the Greek words *photos,* or "light," and *synthesis,* or "putting together." Leaves use the energy from sunlight to put together various raw materials—including water and minerals from the soil, and carbon dioxide from the air—to make food. In other words, leaves are solar-powered food factories.

How do leaves capture the sun's energy? They contain a green chemical substance called chlorophyll. Chlorophyll absorbs sunlight and draws energy from it in a series of chemical reactions. This energy is used to start other chemical reactions through which the raw materials are turned into sugar, starch, cellulose (the main mineral in wood), and even protein.

It is chlorophyll that gives leaves their green color. Leaves also contain other color-producing substances, or pigments. In a few plants, these other pigments may mask the chlorophyll so that the leaves appear red, pink, yellow, or even blue. But the chlorophyll is still there, capturing sunlight for food production.

Because sunlight is essential for photosynthesis, a plant's leaves are generally arranged to catch the most light possible. Often, for example, leaves are set in a spiral around the plant stem. This arrangement prevents the upper leaves from shading those below, so that all can receive sunlight.

The larger the plant, the more food it needs. A full-grown oak tree may have as many as 700,000 leaves—all busily churning out food to help the tree grow and produce its flowers and seeds.

LEAVES THAT SAVE WATER

Some leaves have special features that help them in food production or in some of the other roles that they play. For example, a leaf may be designed to save water, which is essential for photosynthesis and also for the life of the plant. Water evaporates through tiny pores on the surface of leaves, so basking in the sun all day can create quite a risk—the leaf may overheat or lose so much water that it dries out.

To help prevent this, some leaves are covered with fine hairs. The hairs grow most commonly on the undersides of leaves, but some plant leaves are hairy on both sides. The hairs trap moisture and hold it next to the leaf surface. They also act as insulation, protecting the leaf from extremes of heat and cold and shading it from the strongest rays of the sun.

Plants that live in very hot and dry regions must take even more steps to save water. Many of these plants are succulents—they have thick, fleshy tissues that can store water. Cacti are the most famous succulent plants. In most cacti, the leaves have developed into needle-like spines—it is the plant stem that stores water and carries on photosynthesis. But other plants have succulent leaves that are fleshy, water-storing lobes. And the leaves of certain orchids have a bulbous base that acts like a water tank for the plant.

The leaves of the tropical bromeliad form a cup that traps water. And their bright red color lures insects.

The tropical plants called bromeliads trap water in another way. These plants grow in the rain forests—not in the soil but high in the branches of trees. They can't get water through their roots, which often dangle in the air. Instead, the leaves of the plant form a cup that catches rainwater and holds it. The bromeliad then absorbs the water through special leaf hairs.

LEAVES THAT MIMIC FLOWERS

The leaves of many types of bromeliads play still another role: They attract insects

Some plants have specialized leaves called bracts that look just like flower petals. In this tropical anthurium, the bracts have developed into a bright red, waxy sheath called a spathe. It's hard to believe that this exotic "flower" is actually a leaf.

to the plant. In most plants, this is the job of the flowers. Insects that are drawn to the flowers' bright colors and sweet nectar pollinate the plant and so help it reproduce. In certain bromeliads, however, the flowers are small and inconspicuous. But just before the plant blooms, the leaves around the flower turn a brilliant red—designed to catch the eye of any insect.

Other plants use similar tricks. For example, most flowering plants have tiny specialized leaves called bracts at the base of each flower. But in some plants, the bracts develop until they look just like flower petals. For instance, what we think of as the flowers of the dogwood tree are actually groups of large white bracts. The true flowers are small and hard to see.

Many tropical plants, including the poinsettia, have brilliant petal-like bracts. In some, the bracts develop into a waxy sheath (called a spathe) that surrounds part of the flower. The forms and colors can be so exotic that it's hard to believe these bracts and spathes are really leaves.

Usually, plants with petal-like leaves attract insects for pollination. But some plants use their leaves to lure insects for nourishment. The Venus's-flytrap, the sundew, and the pitcher plant are among plants that trap insects and digest them. Not only are their leaves often colored to look like flowers, they may even produce nectar.

Insect-eating plants also depend on their leaves for the capture of their prey. The leaves of pitcher plants form deep cups from which insects can't escape. Those of the sundew have hairs that bear a gluelike substance in which insects become stuck. And the leaves of the Venus's-flytrap are sensitive to touch—when an insect lands, the leaf snaps shut around it and begins to secrete digestive juices.

Some bromeliads benefit from the insects they attract in both ways. Besides pollinating the plant, insects that are drawn to the plant's colorful leaves may fall into the cup of water the leaves contain. The insects drown, and the plant gets the nutrients that are left when they decompose.

LEAVES THAT PROTECT

A plant may attract insects for still another reason: protection. This is particularly common in the tropical rain forests, where hungry leaf mites, caterpillars, and other leaf eaters are constantly chewing on plants. Tender new leaves are especially vulnerable. So some plants enlist allies in their fight for survival—they try to attract ants that will prey on the leaf-eating insects.

Some of these plants have special leaves that provide homes for the ants. The leaves may be shaped into domes or have cavities that shelter the plant's insect allies. Other plant leaves attract the ants by producing sweet nectar, which the ants eat. The nectar-producing organs may even develop and begin to attract ants before the rest of the leaf unfolds. In this way new leaves are protected when they are tender and most in danger from leaf-eating insects.

The leaves of many plants have prickly or razor-sharp edges to discourage grazing animals. Other plants have leaves that produce irritating oils—poison ivy and poison oak are among the best known. And sometimes leaf hairs help a plant from predators. The leaf hairs of the nettle, for example, carry a poison and deliver a burning sting to anyone or anything that touches the leaf.

LEAVES WITH SPECIAL JOBS

The plant world contains many other kinds of specialized leaves. The bulb of an onion, for example, is actually made up of thick, fleshly leaves. The thin, curling tendrils that allow climbing vines to hang on to their supports are also specially adapted leaves.

There are even leaves that can produce new plants. Leaves cut from sedum and from some African violets will take root, and a new plant will develop. In a few other plants, such as the kalanchoe, tiny new plants may form along the edges of mature leaves.

It's plain that the leaves of a plant are more than just green background material. With the unlimited roles they play, leaves are one of the marvels of nature.

Some plants use their leaves to lure insects for nourishment. This sundew plant has sticky hairlike leaves that an unsuspecting damselfly might become greatly attached to.

Meerkats are little African animals that can stand on their hind legs for hours in the sun. Their upright stance may look comical, but it's an important trick the animals use to survive.

UNITED THEY STAND

The meerkat is one animal that's clearly willing to stand up and be counted. In fact, this clever and courageous little creature stands upright on its hind legs for hours at a time, braving the hot African sun. The meerkat's upright stance looks comical—but it helps the animal to survive.

The meerkat has another name—suricate. But "meerkat" is the better-known term. *Meerkat* means "marsh cat" in Afrikaans, a language spoken in South Africa. But don't be fooled by the name—meerkats don't live in marshes, and they aren't cats. And although they look a little like slimmed-down prairie dogs, they are actually members of the mongoose family.

Meerkats live in semidesert areas of southern Africa. Life is hard in these dry areas, and there are many predators that would like nothing better than to dine on a tasty little meerkat. The secret of the meerkat's success is simple: teamwork. These animals live in colonies, and they cooperate in every aspect of life, from finding food to raising their young.

MEERKATS ON GUARD

A meerkat is roughly the size of a large squirrel. Its body is about 1 foot (30 centimeters) long, and its tapering tail is only a bit shorter than that. The coarse, gray-brown fur has a yellowish tinge, with brownish bands along the back and on the tail. The ears and the tip of the tail are black. Dark-rimmed eyes, a pointy nose, sharp teeth, and long, powerful claws complete the picture.

Bands of meerkats live in underground burrows, which they sometimes share in a friendly fashion with ground squirrels and other animals. With their long claws, the meerkats are excellent diggers. The tunnels and chambers of their burrows may extend many yards and have several different entrances. There may be as many as 30 meerkats in a clan, but many groups have fewer members.

The meerkats come tumbling out of their burrows at sunrise and start the day with one of their favorite activities: a sunbath. The animals stand together in a group, with their bellies turned toward the warming rays of the sun. Soon, however, the meerkats begin the day's work—an endless search for the insects, lizards, eggs, plant bulbs, and small rodents, snakes, and birds that they love to eat.

Meerkats hunt for food in groups, ranging over a territory that may cover several miles. The group hunts in a different section of the territory each day. When they have exhausted the food supply, which may take months, they will move to a new territory and dig a new burrow.

As they scurry along on all fours, meerkats constantly sniff and scratch the dry ground and explore every nook and cranny, looking for tasty morsels. When a meerkat sniffs out a beetle or some other tidbit, it digs furiously until it has found the prize. Only when the prey is completely uncovered does the meerkat kill and eat it.

During this single-minded pursuit of food, the meerkat is all but defenseless, with its head and claws buried in the ground. If a predator should come along, the meerkat would be an easy mark. This is where teamwork—and the upright stance—comes in.

When a group of meerkats goes hunting, at least one will always act as a guard. This meerkat will stand up and scan the area con-

stantly, looking for jackals and other predators on the ground and for eagles and vultures in the sky. Meerkats have keen noses and excellent eyesight, and they can spot eagles that are no more than specks in the sky.

Although they aren't very good climbers, meerkats willingly clamber onto rocks and up trees to get a better view when they are on guard. And they don't seem to mind standing upright, even up on their toes, for long periods of time. The meerkat's tail is an important asset in this: When the animal stands upright, it stiffens its tail and uses it for support.

Meerkats make good baby-sitters, too. While a mother meerkat hunts for food, another adult will stay with her babies—tending, grooming, and cuddling the youngsters.

The meerkats take turns on guard duty, so that all have a chance to eat. When the guard meerkat senses danger, it utters a long warning peep or bark. The other animals quickly run for cover.

What if there's no cover handy? Then the meerkats stand and fight. These little animals can be surprisingly fierce. They bunch together in a tight formation, fluff out their fur, arch their backs, stick their tails up in the air, and start to growl and hiss. Then, together, they advance on their enemy in a stiff-legged gait, jumping into the air with each stride. The effect is quite alarming—many predators run off. But if the predator stands its ground, the meerkats continue to advance, screaming and hissing at their enemy. They may even bite.

Meerkats prefer to run from large predators and from very dangerous ones, such as eagles. But they often gang up on smaller ones, including snakes, to drive them out of the territory. The group behaves in much the same way when it meets rival meerkats that are trying to enter its territory. After such an encounter, the meerkats in the victorious group may mill around excitedly for a few minutes, chattering and hugging each other.

As the day gets hotter, the meerkats seek out the shade of a bush or tree. While one of the group, as always, stands guard, the others sit or lie down to rest. They may cuddle or groom each other in the shade. Those that have the energy may play, tumbling rowdily in the dirt.

At the end of the day, the meerkats return to their burrow for the night. One by one they crawl in, pile on top of each other, and curl up. Finally, a mound of meerkats is sleeping soundly.

BABY-SITTERS

Hunting and defense aren't the only activities in which meerkats cooperate. The group works together to raise the young of any member. Baby meerkats are born in litters, usually of two to five. Their ears and eyes are closed for the first ten to fourteen days of life, and they stay in the burrow. The mother nurses them. But other meerkats help—by baby-sitting. While the mother goes out with the group to forage for food, another adult will stay with the babies, often

"Say a few words for your fans," scientist David Macdonald seems to be asking. Researchers would like to learn more about meerkats, especially about how they communicate with each other. These animals make a wide variety of sounds; some are danger signals, but many of the other sounds are still unidentified.

for the entire day. Other adults also help to groom and cuddle the young.

By the time young meerkats are six weeks old, the mother has begun to bring them food. They learn about solid food by snatching bits from her mouth. In fact, the young often won't consider eating even the tastiest morsel unless they've first obtained it in this way from their mother.

As they get older, the young go out with the group on foraging expeditions. Each young meerkat tags along with an older animal, learning the ins and outs of hunting. Although adult meerkats don't generally share the food they find with other adults, they seem willingly to share it with the youngsters.

OBSERVING MEERKATS

Because meerkats have a limited range, they haven't been studied extensively. They are best known in South Africa, where they are sometimes kept as pets. A pet meerkat is a wonderful way to keep mice and other rodents in check.

Recently, however, scientists have begun to learn about the complex social structure that meerkats have in the wild. They have already observed that the structure in a meerkat group is different from the structure in wolf packs and some other animal groups. A wolf pack, for example, has a strict social order, from the pack leader down to the lowest, weakest wolf. Meerkats seem to enjoy much more equal status, and they cooperate more than wolves do. Some spend more time baby-sitting or on guard duty than others, but everyone takes a turn.

Scientists would also like to learn more about the way these animals communicate with each other. Meerkats make a wide variety of sounds—murmurs, grunts, barks, peeps, trills, growls, and shrieks. Some are clearly danger signals, and others are just as clearly meant to frighten off enemies. But many of the sounds are unidentified.

It's likely that researchers will enjoy finding the answsers to these questions. Clever, comical, and full of spunk, meerkats would make any scientist smile.

BATMANIA

In the summer of 1989, people went bats —over Batman, one of the most famous comic-book characters of all time. The occasion for all the excitement was the release of a new feature-length motion picture about this legendary masked crime-fighter. The year also marked an important anniversary for Batman's fans: Exactly 50 years earlier, in 1939, the Batman character had appeared in his very first comic-book adventure.

Batman's fans know his legend by heart: By day, he's a millionaire man-about-town who goes by the name Bruce Wayne. But at night, he puts on a bat-mask and cape to do battle with a whole gallery of evil criminals —the Joker, Penguin, and others. In many adventures, Batman is accompanied by a sidekick, Robin. His home is Gotham City. His base is a bat-filled cave. And he rockets around in a special car, the Batmobile.

That basic story has appeared in many different forms. From his first comic-book adventure (called "The Case of the Chemical Syndicate") in the May, 1939, issue of Detective Comics, Batman graduated to comic books of his own. Batman movie serials were popular with Saturday matinee audiences in the 1940's. And in the 1960's, Batman's adventures were the subject of a hit television series. Naturally, the "look" of the character and the specifics of his adventures changed many times over the years.

The 1989 motion picture *Batman* filled in some of the background of Batman's early years. The film told, for example, how Bruce Wayne had decided to devote his life to fighting crime after seeing his parents killed during a robbery. It told how the masked crimefighter had later begun his rivalry with the arch criminal who became known as the Joker. And it explained how the Joker got his evil, leering grin, his green hair, and his pasty white complexion: They were the results of a fall into a vat full of poisonous chemicals.

In many ways, the 1989 film also returned to the mood of the original 1939 comic-book adventures, which had a dark and mysterious tone. Gotham City was shown as a brooding, sinister place. In this city, tall buildings shut out the light and made the streets dark even during the day. Batman's sidekick Robin was nowhere to be seen (Robin's character hadn't been invented in 1939). Instead, Batman pursued the Joker with news photographer Vicki Vale (played by actress Kim Basinger) at his side.

As played by actor Jack Nicholson, the Joker fairly dripped evil. But to play the part of Batman, the moviemakers made a choice that some fans found a bit surprising. Batman's original comic-book creator, Bob Kane, had drawn the character as a strapping, muscular, square-jawed superhero. But in the motion picture, the title role was played by actor Michael Keaton, who didn't have any of these characteristics and was a much more human figure.

Still, when Keaton put on the Batman costume, he looked the part. And as *Batman* developed into one of the year's biggest hits, it was clear that the fans approved. Soon after the film opened in June, it began to set new box-office records for ticket sales around the country.

The popularity of the motion picture soon led to a boom in sales of Batman-related items, too. Batman comic books suddenly became more popular than ever. And Batman toys appeared in stores. Many toys were based on props that had been used in the film. There was even an electric-powered toy Batmobile, just big enough for kids to ride in, that was based on the car that had been designed for the motion picture.

Batman logos and designs began to pop up everywhere—on caps, T-shirts, jackets, posters, buttons, mugs, stickers, and more. And items that featured the Joker and his evil grin were reported to be selling just as quickly as those that featured Batman himself. On the 50th anniversary of the legendary comic-book hero's creation, Batmania swept the land.

The popularity of the 1989 film *Batman* helped produce a wave of "Batmania." Sales of Batman comics, toys, buttons, T-shirts, posters, and other items soared.

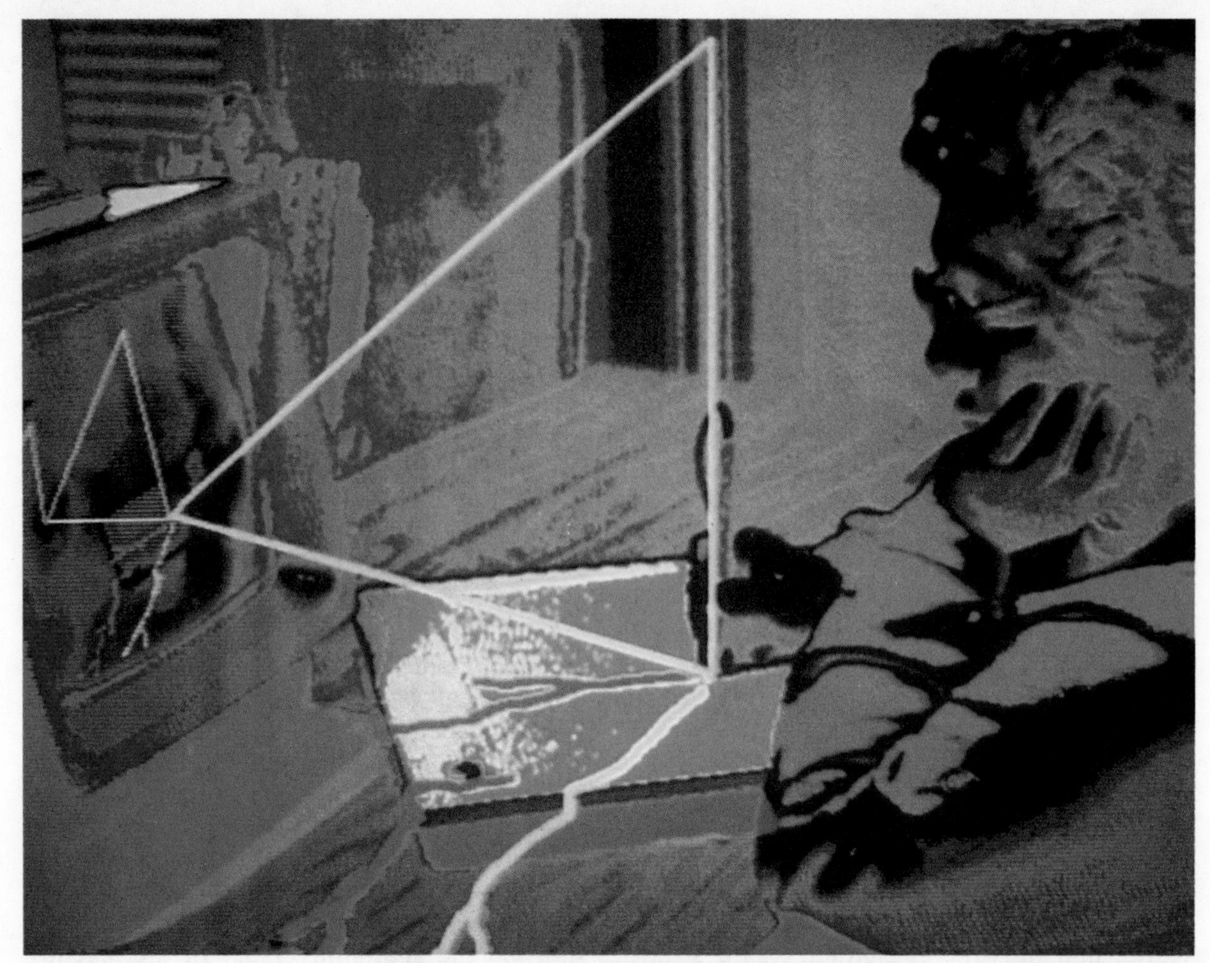

Computers are now providing artists with a new medium—a sort of electronic easel and palette. Artists, and designers and filmmakers too, can use computers to produce a variety of new effects. (The computer drawing above is called *Drawing in Time*.)

THE CREATIVE COMPUTER

Computers are designed to perform complex mathematical calculations, store and sort large amounts of information, and handle other tiresome and time-consuming chores. Most people don't think of these machines in terms of art or creativity. But increasingly, computers are becoming creative tools: With computer graphics techniques, artists can produce images by computer.

Computer graphics techniques were first developed mainly for scientific purposes. Using these techniques, scientists have been able to create images of things that are too far away or too small to see—the surface of distant planets, the structures of molecules. The scientist simply enters all the information about the planet or the molecule into the computer, and the computer uses the information to produce an image.

Computer graphics have also become important in medicine, mapmaking, agriculture, industrial design and manufacturing, and many other fields. The images produced for these uses are often quite artistic. But their main purpose is to show technical or scientific information in a visual way.

Now, however, artists have begun to realize that a computer can provide them with a new medium—a sort of electronic easel and palette. A computer can eliminate many of the more tedious tasks that go into the creation of a drawing or painting, and it can allow the artist to produce a range of new effects.

Designers and filmmakers, too, have discovered that computer graphics can open up new creative worlds. And 1989 was an especially important year for computer animation: *Tin Toy,* a short animated film, became the first computer-generated film to win an Academy Award.

HOW IT'S DONE

Computer graphics vary greatly, depending on the sort of computer equipment and the programs (instructions that tell the machine what to do) that are used. But no matter how simple or sophisticated they are, most computer graphics systems have certain features in common.

The inside surface of a computer screen is coated with tiny dots of light-sensitive chemicals called phosphors. The dots are arranged in rows to form a grid that covers the screen, making the screen somewhat like a sheet of graph paper. Each dot is called a picture element, or pixel for short. Using a computer graphics program, the artist tells the computer which pixels to turn on, or light up. And glowing pixels create the image on the screen.

The amount of detail in the image depends on the number of pixels on the screen. Most home computers have comparatively few pixels. Thus the pictures drawn on home screens often have a boxy appearance and show little detail. Diagonal lines and curves may appear jagged or stepped. But more powerful computers may have millions of pixels on the screen. With these machines, it's possible to draw flowing lines and highly detailed pictures.

In addition, some computers can be programmed to blend the sharp edges of images for a more realistic look. They can be told to shade images, so that the forms appear three dimensional. And they can be instructed to produce the kind of sketching strokes that a human hand might make or the brushstrokes made by different kinds and sizes of brushes.

Computer images can also be produced in a full range of colors. For this, the screen must have phosphors that will glow in the three primary colors of light—red, blue, and green. These color phosphors are turned on in various combinations to produce all the colors that an artist might need. When red and green phosphors are turned on together, for example, they produce a yellow light.

To "draw" on a computer screen, an artist delivers instructions to the machine in several ways. Some instructions (especially those for color and shading) may be typed into the computer on a keyboard. Or the artist may use a hand control called a mouse. And in many computer graphics systems, the artist draws with a pen or stylus on a special tablet. The tablet detects the pen moving across its surface, and it transmits the instructions to the computer in an electronic code.

Some systems use a different device, called a light pen. With this instrument, the artist draws directly on the computer screen. The pen is plugged into the computer, and it turns on pixels wherever it touches the screen.

Other devices will produce images of three-dimensional objects. In one technique, called mapping, the artist can use a special wand to trace over the surface of an object, and an image of the object will appear on the screen.

When the artist is finished with the image, a printer attached to the computer can produce a picture on paper. Or, using other computer attachments, it's possible to transfer the finished image onto film.

An artist can use a computer to produce a work that is an abstract fantasy, such as *Circus* by Barbara Joffe.

PAINTING BY PIXEL

For artists, computers offer a number of advantages over sketchpads and easels. If an artist wants to change colors or even parts of the design, a computer can make the changes at the touch of a button—there's no need to erase or to begin again on a fresh sheet of paper. Colors can be toned down or made more intense just as easily. Objects can be moved around. And if the artist doesn't like the new look, it's simple to change back to the original version or to try something else.

In some sophisticated systems, the artist can instruct the computer to show light falling on objects from a certain angle. The computer can also change the surface textures of objects and the way they reflect light. Or the artist can program the computer to create random curves and jagged lines—to produce natural-looking gullies in a landscape, for example.

Computers can also produce unusual effects that are difficult to achieve with traditional artists' media such as paper and paint. Objects can be made to seem translucent or to glow with vibrant color. Some systems can produce an extraordinary range of colors—one graphics program can create 16 million different shades.

A sculptor can use a computer to preview a work before it is made. Suppose, for example, that a sculptor wants to make a large marble statue. Before a single cut is made in the marble, many sketches and clay models of the figure will be made. But a computer can shorten this work. Many graphics systems can be given information about a three-dimensional object and then will produce views of the object from almost any angle. In this way the artist can see what the sculpture will look like from all sides, and changes can be made before the work begins.

Artists who use computers say that these mechanical devices don't detract from creativity. On the contrary—computer technology helps the artist become more creative. An artist can use a computer to produce a work that is a dreamlike, abstract fantasy or as realistic as a photograph. It's not surprising that more and more artists are working with computers, or that art and design schools have begun to include computer instruction in their offerings.

A computer artist can also produce a work that's as realistic as a photograph, such as this still from the computer-animated film *Red's Dream*.

In 1989, *Tin Toy* became the first computer-animated film to win an Academy Award.

AUTOMATED ANIMATION

Some of the most exciting developments in computer graphics are taking place in the field of animation. In animated films, creating the illusion of movement can be a painstaking and time-consuming job. Suppose, for example, that a character is to take one step forward. To look smooth and natural, the step must be stretched over many frames of film. Each frame is like a still photograph, but when they are run together the effect is one of motion.

In traditional animated films, each frame must be drawn separately by hand. But with a computer, the animator can make one image at the start of the step and one at the end. The computer will produce all the frames needed in between. The computer can also be instructed to fill in all the colors, shading, and highlights needed in the scene.

The most sophisticated computer animation systems, like the one used to make the award-winning short *Tin Toy,* take this process even further. *Tin Toy* is about a baby named Billy and a wind-up toy named Tinny. All the images appear three-dimensional. For Billy, the filmmakers first made a clay model of the baby. Then they "mapped" the model—traced over its surface with a computer wand—and the computer constructed its own three-dimensional image.

Once this image was stored in the computer, the filmmakers could instruct the machine to animate it. They were able to create highly detailed effects, including a wide range of facial expressions. As the character moved about, the computer made all the needed changes in perspective, shadows, and highlights. Each surface in the film—the baby's skin, the cardboard and cellophane of the toy's box—was given a lifelike texture. The computer even duplicated the effect of the sun streaming through a window and being reflected off these surfaces.

Fully computerized animated films like *Tin Toy* are rare because they are so expensive to produce. But the same techniques have been widely used to fill in backgrounds in traditional animated films and to create short segments, such as animated television ads. Computer animation has also been used to create special effects for feature films. Instead of building and filming a model of a spacecraft for a science-fiction film, for example, it's now possible to create a three-dimensional animated spaceship on a computer.

Filmmakers say that in animation, computers are the wave of the future—production costs will drop as the equipment and techniques become more widely available. Meanwhile, computer graphics techniques are being used in other areas of the movie industry. For example, computers are used to "colorize" (add color to) old black-and-white films. In this technique, an artist uses a computer to add color to a few frames of each scene. The computer stores the color information and uses it to color in the rest of the frames for that scene.

The future may hold even more surprising developments in computerized filmmaking. One experimental program uses techniques similar to those used in *Tin Toy* to create animated images of actors. The program's creators say that it could be used to change details of actors' expressions after filming, to synchronize dubbed foreign-language films (so that the sound and lip movement would match), to bring famous actors of the past back to the screen in new roles, and even to create entirely new—and artificial—screen personalities.

GREAT GRAPHICS

You may not realize it, but computer graphics are all around you. For example, computers are used to create many of the graphics that accompany television news programs. Their great advantage in this work is speed. Once images have been created in a computer, they can be stored there as well. Then the artist can quickly call them up and combine them in new ways.

Suppose that the night's news includes a report of a terrorist attack at an airport. Using a computer, the artist can call up a map locating the airport, add a previously created symbol for an explosion, and even combine words with the picture. All this can be done in minutes instead of the hours it would take to create a new piece of art.

Advertisers and product and package designers are also making more and more use of computer graphics systems. Some systems not only let a designer see what a product or package will look like from all angles, they also show what it will look like when it's placed on a store shelf, surrounded by other products. The designer can see the product just as the customer will see it.

Computers will never replace paper, pencils, paints, and other artists' tools, But as these machines become even more sophisticated, it's likely that they will play a larger and larger role in all kinds of creative work.

COMPUTER CONCERTO

Just as computers have invaded the world of art and film, so they have invaded the world of music. Electronic recording and amplification techniques have been around for a long time. But today new computerized devices are changing the way music is written and performed.

Some musicians and composers are making use of "smart" amplifiers that alter the sounds produced by traditional musical instruments. An example of the sort of creative work that can be done with computerized amplification is *Répons,* a concerto work by the composer Pierre Boulez. In *Répons,* the sounds of eight solo instruments are picked up by microphones and passed through a computer. The computer extends, alters, and repeats the sounds, routing them to different speakers placed around the concerto hall. The result is that the music seems to reverberate all around the audience.

Music synthesizers, which mimic the sounds of musical instruments, have also become more sophisticated. And when one of these devices is plugged into a computer, a musician can use the computer to compose music. The computer can be instructed to play the composition back on the synthesizer. And when the computer is satisfied with the piece, the notes can be printed out.

The most advanced computer-synthesizers can realistically reproduce the sounds of almost any instrument—and some noninstrumental sounds as well. Most synthesizers make use of a keyboard, like the keyboard of a piano. But one type looks, sounds, and is played like a saxaphone, responding to mouth as well as finger movements. It mimics the breathy sound of wind instruments, but it can also create the sounds of other instruments.

There's even a synthesizer that can turn the sound of a voice into the sound of various instruments. And computers are making progress in mimicking the human voice itself—the most difficult instrument of all. In the future, they may be able to duplicate the voices of famous singers of the past to improve the voices of living singers. For instance, a computer that matched a singer's voice could hold notes at higher or lower levels than the singer could. Then the sounds of the natural and artificial voices could be blended together.

Sophisticated computers can perform some amazing musical feats. One experimental system can take the place of a human accompanist—playing the piano background for a violin sonata, for example. The computer is first programmed with all the information about the sonata. Then, as it plays the piano part through the synthesizer, it "listens" to the violinist and adjusts its speed to match the musician's. It can even skip ahead and catch up if the musician makes a mistake and misses a few notes.

In the future, you may hear musical sounds that have never been heard before—the sounds of new instruments created by computers. And instruments may take new shapes and be played in new ways. Some people envision musical wands that will simply be waved in different patterns to produce different sounds. Or musicians may create symphonies by running their hands over a pressure-sensitive dome connected to a computer. It's even possible that a computer will "read" listeners' responses to music by registering their facial expressions and body movements. Then the computer will change the music to fit the audience's response.

DISNEY MAGIC

Did you ever wonder how animators make characters like Roger Rabbit and Mickey Mouse come to life on the screen? How moviemakers create explosions, hurricanes, and death-defying stunts? What it would be like to see your favorite TV show taped in the studio—or even to star in a TV show?

You can find out—and have a lot of fun at the same time—at the Disney-MGM Studios Theme Park. The park, which opened on May 1, 1989, is one of several new additions at Walt Disney World, the sprawling Florida complex that includes Disney's Magic Kingdom and Epcot Center.

MOVIE MAGIC

Disney-MGM Studios takes motion pictures and television as its theme. It's almost a re-creation of Hollywood, with all the glamour and excitement of the famous California movie capital. In fact, Disney-MGM Studios is more than a theme park—it's a working movie and television studio. Among the projects that have been made there are the film *Ernest Saves Christmas* and the television series *Superboy*.

But most of the attractions are designed to delight visitors and give them an inside look at the fascinating world of movie and television production. The Hollywood atmosphere is everywhere. When you step through the main entrance of the park, you're on Hollywood Boulevard—a street inspired by the Hollywood street of the same name as it appeared in the 1930's. All around you are buildings in the Art Deco and "California Crazy" styles of the movie capital.

As you stroll past the shops and restaurants, don't be surprised if an autograph hound (actually a park employee) stops you and asks for your autograph. You may even spot a celebrity—film and television stars often mingle with the crowd. And there are handprints and footprints of movie stars in the concrete sidewalk outside the Chinese Theater (just as there are in the concrete sidewalk outside the famous Chinese Theater in Hollywood).

The Chinese Theater is the centerpiece of the park and also the entrance to one of the major attractions: The Great Movie Ride. Hop aboard a tram, and the ride will carry you back into movie history—straight into your favorite films. Life-size animated figures appear in scenes from *The Wizard of Oz, Mary Poppins, Casablanca, Raiders of the Lost Ark,* and other movie classics. Here you'll see Tarzan swinging through the jungle, gangsters shooting it out in a Chicago back alley, and even the hair-raising monster from the movie *Alien*.

From your tour of movies of the past, you can go on to see how the movies of today are created—and maybe see a film or TV show actually being made. The Backstage Studio Tour takes you through Disney-MGM Studios' production facilities. Along the way, guides and short films (starring Bill Cosby, Warren Beatty, and other well-known actors) explain the moviemaking process. You visit a soundstage, where stars, directors, and technicians pool their talents to create films and television shows. And you tour the complex post-production facilities, where computers and other sophisticated equipment put the finishing touches on films.

A tram tour takes you through a studio back lot, past mock streets from a residential suburb (including the house used in the TV show *The Golden Girls*) and New York City

Gangsters prowl a back alley in the Great Movie Ride, which takes you back in movie history.

(the skyscrapers are actually small, but movie-making magic makes them look tall on film). Hang on to your seat as the tram enters Catastrophe Canyon. Here the ground is suddenly rocked by an earthquake. An oil tank erupts in a fireball. And a torrential flash flood sweeps down toward your tram. But visitors are safe—it's all done through the magic of special effects.

You'll find out how moviemakers create more special effects—sea battles and windstorms, for example—as your tour continues. (Another attraction, Star Tours, is set to open early in 1990. It promises a spectacular show of breathtaking effects like those used in *Star Wars* and other space adventure films.) And if you want to see death-defying stunts, take a seat for the Indiana Jones Epic Stunt Spectacular. After professionals dodge fire, steam, bubbling lava, and flying boulders, volunteers from the audience get a chance to try some scary-looking stunts.

You can get even more closely involved in production when you visit one of the park's most popular attractions, SuperStar Television. Here visitors form a studio audience, and volunteers are chosen to act out roles in episodes of famous television shows—*Cheers, I Love Lucy, General Hospital, Gilligan's Island,* and others. As the volunteers act their roles, the production crew uses the latest TV technology to insert their images into the actual episode. To the audience watching on television monitors, the volunteers seem to be starring in the show.

The Monster Sound Show is another hands-on production experience. Here you'll see technicians use sophisticated equipment to add sound effects to a comedy thriller—footsteps, thunder, a knock at the door. Then audience volunteers try their hands at the equipment, often with unexpected (and funny) results. And they have a chance to dub their voices into film clips featuring Clark Gable and other stars of the past.

Of course, animation is what first made Walt Disney famous. It's natural, then, that one of the most popular attractions at the Disney-MGM Studios Theme Park offers a behind-the-scenes look at the creation of animated films. At The Magic of Disney Animation, visitors see films and exhibits that explain the steps in putting together an ani-

MAKE ROOM FOR MISS PIGGY

The family of Disney characters welcomed some new members in 1989: Miss Piggy, Kermit the Frog, Fozzie Bear, and the rest of the Muppet troupe. In August, the Walt Disney Company announced that it would acquire Henson Associates, the company that owns these popular puppet characters. The Muppets were created by puppeteer Jim Henson in the 1950's. (Henson also created Big Bird and other characters that appear on the television show *Sesame Street,* but these weren't included in the sale.) Since then, the Muppets have starred in their own live-action television show and appeared in feature-length films and animated cartoons. Now Miss Piggy and the other Muppets will continue their show-business careers as part of the Disney Group, and they'll appear alongside Mickey Mouse and Donald Duck at Disney theme parks.

mated feature, from the first rough sketches to the finished film. And they can watch actual Disney animators as the artists work on their imaginative creations.

It all adds up to an exciting experience—a fascinating behind-the-scenes look at the magical world of film and television.

. . . AND MORE

The Disney-MGM Studios Theme Park wasn't the only new attraction at Walt Disney World in 1989. Summer saw the opening of Typhoon Lagoon, a 56-acre water park that's packed with thrills. Along with sandy beaches and a tropical setting, Typhoon Lagoon has nine water slides and the world's largest inland surfing lagoon, with mechanically generated waves. If you prefer quieter attractions, you can go snorkeling in a special pool that's stocked with brightly colored tropical fish (and even a few harmless, but spooky looking, sharks). Or you can grab an inner tube and float down a creek, through a hidden grotto and a tropical rain forest.

There were new attractions at the other Walt Disney World parks, too. At the Magic Kingdom, a new adventure called Dreamflight traces the history of flight. Through computer-animated film, visitors are put right in cockpits of various aircraft, from early planes to high-speed jets of the future.

Late in the year, Wonders of Life opened at Epcot Center. Under a huge golden dome, this pavilion showcases a number of attractions dealing with fitness and the way the human body works. In "Body Wars," for example, visitors take a fast-paced simulated trip through the human bloodstream and watch as the body's immune system fights off infection. In "Cranium Command," life-size animated figures combine with film to give an inside view of the way the brain works. And at "Fitness Fairgrounds," visitors go through a fun house based on the five senses and get computerized analyses of their general health.

The Disney company calls the people who dream up these attractions Imagineers. What will the Imagineers think up next? Well, in 1989 plans were being made for Euro Disneyland, a new theme park to be built on a site outside Paris, France. When this park opens in 1992, it will join Walt Disney World, the original Disneyland in California, and Tokyo Disneyland in Japan in spreading Disney magic around the world.

On a tour of production facilities, you can star in a "Bee" movie—and, through the magic of special effects, see yourself fly through the air on the back of a bee.

EARTHQUAKE!

It was four minutes past five, and another workday was coming to an end in San Francisco, California. Traffic was building up on bridges and freeways around the city. At Candlestick Park, home of the San Francisco Giants, an excited crowd packed the stadium for the third game of the World Series.

Suddenly, the ground began to rumble and shake. Buildings and bridges swayed and cracked, sending chunks of concrete, brick, and glass raining into the streets. Cars bounced around like toys as the ground moved up and down in waves. On the main bridge leading across San Francisco Bay to Oakland, a section of roadway collapsed. In Oakland, the top deck of a freeway crashed down onto the lower deck, crushing cars beneath it. Power went out, and as night fell the sky reflected the reddish glow of fire.

The earthquake that struck the San Francisco area on October 17, 1989, measured 7.1 on the Richter scale of ground motion. It was the most powerful quake in the United States in 25 years. At least 67 people died, and more than 1,400 were injured. Damage was estimated at more than $6 billion.

Earthquakes are a fact of life in San Francisco and in most of coastal California. This region marks the meeting point of two of the great plates that make up the earth's crust. San Francisco sits atop the San Andreas fault—the line where the North American plate meets the Pacific plate.

The earth's plates are slowly but constantly shifting. And where two plates touch, they may rub together and snag. Pressure builds up until, suddenly, the earth snaps along the fault line, releasing the pressure and sending tremors through the ground.

The 1989 quake was centered south of San Francisco, in mountains near Santa Cruz. Damage in Santa Cruz was severe. There and in San Francisco, older buildings were especially vulnerable. But quick action—by firefighters, rescue workers, and ordinary people who helped pull victims from the rubble—kept deaths to a minimum. And many structures, including the Golden Gate Bridge and the skyscrapers of downtown San Francisco, suffered little or no damage.

Even as rebuilding began, however, scientists issued a warning. Plenty of pressure is still pent up along the fault lines that stretch for hundreds of miles along the California coast. Future earthquakes—even larger ones—are likely.

A POLKA-DOT TREE

Scraps of brightly colored paper can grow into leaves and flowers . . . or almost anything else you might want to create. The trick is to turn those scraps of paper into lots and lots of paper dots and then "paint" the dots onto a dark background.

Begin by choosing a design. If you decide to make a tree, you'll need pink, yellow, red, or blue for flowers, and green for foliage. If possible, work with several shades of a color.

Lightly sketch your design onto a paper that will serve as the background. Decide if your picture will consist entirely of dots. An alternative is to use paint or ink for part of the picture. For instance, use white paint to form the trunk and branches of a tree. Do this before adding the dots. If several coats of paint are needed, let each coat dry before adding the next. And by covering part of the tree trunk with several coats of paint, you create a more three-dimensional and bark-like look.

Use a paper punch to make the dots. It will be easier to work with the dots if you keep each color—even each shade—in a separate pile.

Attach the dots to the background paper one at a time. Place a small dot of glue on the paper. Then cover the glue dot with a paper dot. Press down on the paper dot to be certain it's firmly in place.

To make a cluster of flowers, partially overlap a number of dots of different shades. Overlap dots of various shades of green to create a textured ground effect. And for "dotty" trunk and branches, use shades of beige and brown.

Place your finished picture in a frame, or glue it to a heavy piece of cardboard. Attach a hanger to the back and you are ready to display your picture on your wall.

You can also use dot art to make greeting cards and book covers. Abstract and geometric designs might be especially attractive on these. Dot art can even be used for an interesting science project: Make a series of pictures of the Big Dipper and other star constellations using white dots on a black or blue background.

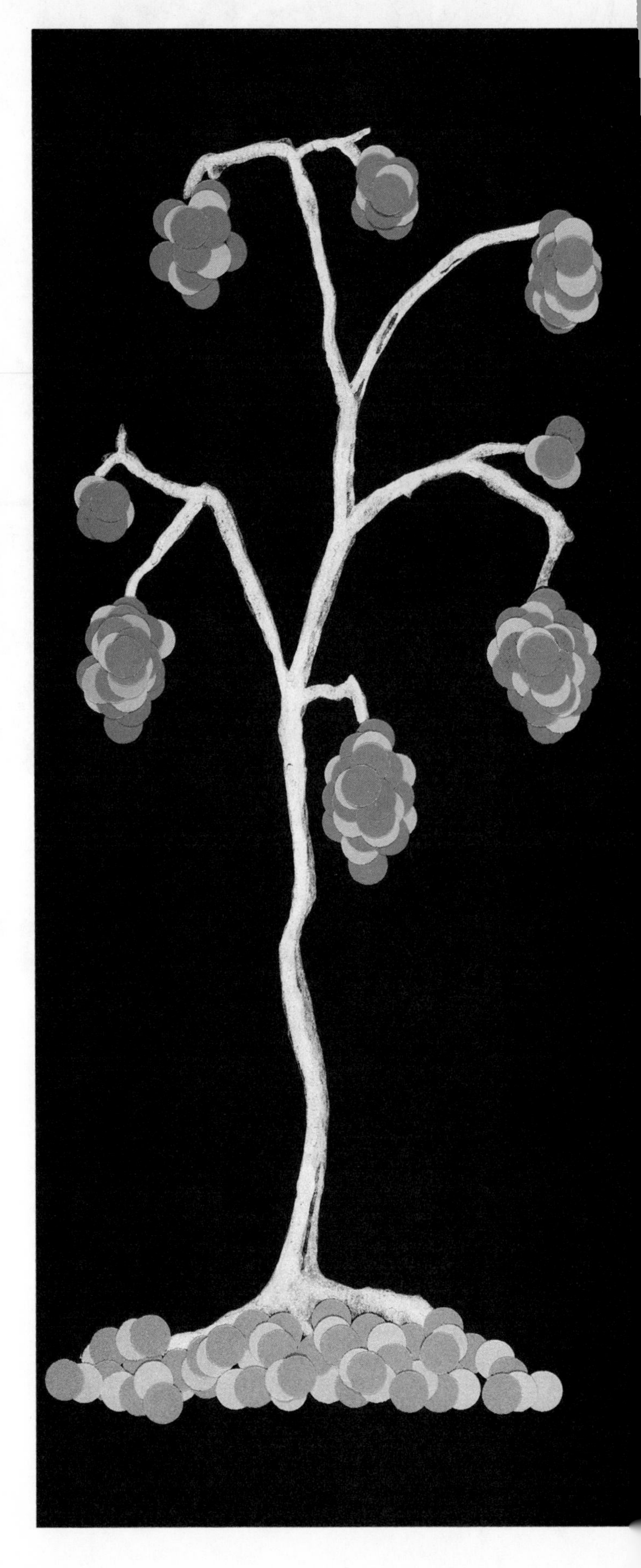

The Temple of Gloom

Mowgli was playing high in a tree when he saw something white in the distance. It was the top of an ancient stone tower.

"Let's go explore it," he called to his friends, Bagheera the panther and Baloo the bear, as he jumped to the ground.

"Oh, no, Mowgli." Bagheera shook his head. "Jungle folk never go near that tower. Legends say that tower is near the lost Temple of Gloom, where the terrible SadStone is hidden."

"The SadStone?" laughed Mowgli.

"Don't scoff," scolded Bagheera. "The SadStone makes everyone who looks at it cry uncontrollably."

"Aw Baggie, you don't believe all that old beeswax, do you?" Baloo looked up from the bananas he was eating. "I don't. And to prove it, I'll go there with Little Britches, here. We'll show you we're not afraid of any old legend."

Ignoring Bagheera's warnings, Mowgli and Baloo started for the tower, singing and laughing as they went.

They didn't know that Kaa, the python, had heard everything they'd said.

"Here'sss a chance to get my coils around Mowgli," Kaa said to himself. He slithered after the happy-go-lucky pair.

"Baloo, I hear something," Mowgli looked around. "It sounds like someone is following us."

Kaa froze and tried to look like a stick.

Baloo just laughed. "It's probably that stuffed shirt, Bagheera, trying to scare us," he said. "Don't pay any attention to him."

"Thisss is going to be easier than I thought," Kaa smiled slyly.

After a long walk, they neared the tower. All around them the jungle was thick and dark, with twisting vines choking the path. Huge trees shut out the sunshine. No birds called overhead. Nothing stirred.

"This place gives me a funny feeling," Baloo said nervously. "And I don't mean a ha-ha funny feeling, either."

Mowgli laughed. "You're starting to sound just like Bagheera," he teased. "Come on, Baloo, where's your sense of humor?" He jumped on Baloo and started to tickle him.

Baloo laughed and wrestled Mowgli to the ground. They rolled in the leaves, squashing the end of Kaa's hidden tail.

"Eech! Ouch!" Kaa winced quietly. "That does it! I'm getting a grip on that Man-cub if it'sss the last thing I do!" he hissed.

Baloo stood up and brushed himself off.

"I still don't like it here," he said. "Let's go." But Mowgli wanted to keep playing. He flung himself at Baloo again.

"Oof!" Baloo tripped over a large stone and sat down hard. Suddenly a loud groaning sound filled the air. The earth shook. Before Mowgli's eyes, a huge hole opened in the ground beneath Baloo.

"Help!" Baloo yelled as he toppled in. He landed far below.

Mowgli leaned over the edge of the deep pit and peered into the inky blackness.

"Baloo! Are you all right?" he called. "Say something!"

Baloo's voice echoed from below. "It's dark down here. I can feel stone walls around me, but I can't see anything."

Baloo felt around. He touched something smooth and cold and covered with mud. When he scraped the mud off, a pale, bluish-white light began to glow inside the pit.

Mowgli looked down. In the strange light, he could see enormous carved stone figures.

As he stared, he heard an odd sound. Baloo was sitting on the floor of the pit, holding an enormous blue jewel shaped like a teardrop. And he was crying!

"Baloo! You must have discovered the Temple of Gloom," Mowgli yelled. "That must be the SadStone you're holding!"

A huge tear slid down Baloo's nose, followed by another, and another. "Oh, this is terrible! I feel awful!" Baloo blubbered. "I can't stop crying." His sobs began to echo through the jungle.

"Don't cry, Baloo! Please stop. I'll get you out of there." Mowgli looked around for something to help Baloo climb out of the pit.

When Kaa saw Mowgli alone, he came out of hiding.

"There ssseems to be sssome trouble," Kaa said as he approached Mowgli. He tried to make Mowgli look him in the eyes. "Perhapsss I can be of some asssistance?"

Mowgli knew that if he looked Kaa in the eyes, Kaa would hypnotize him. Instead he stared at Kaa's long, long tail. And it gave him an idea.

"Oh, Kaa! I'm so glad to see you!" he said, still staring at Kaa's tail. As he talked, he began slowly walking backward.

"You are?" Kaa was pleased. No one was ever glad to see him. He slithered toward Mowgli. Mowgli backed up more. Slowly, carefully, the Man-cub began to circle a nearby tree trunk. Kaa followed every step.

"I'll bet there's no one in the jungle longer than you, Kaa," Mowgli said. He kept moving until the end of Kaa's tail was wrapped all the way around the tree.

"That'sss true," Kaa smiled.

Quickly Mowgli bent down and tied a huge knot in Kaa's tail. Kaa was fastened to the tree!

"Why, you little shrimp!" Kaa hissed. "I'll get you for that!" He lunged at Mowgli.

But Mowgli leaped out of reach. He grabbed a vine and swung out over the deep pit where Baloo sat bawling.

Kaa lunged again, straight out over the pit.

"Aaahhh!" Kaa screeched as he missed

Mowgli and crashed into the pit. There he hung, upside down, with his tail tied firmly to the tree, and his head dangling near Baloo.

"Quick, Baloo!" Mowgli called. "Toss me the SadStone. Then climb up Kaa like a rope."

Still sniffling, Baloo threw the SadStone out of the pit. It landed with a thump and rolled into a pile of leaves.

Baloo began to climb up Kaa, who began to twist and squirm furiously. But Baloo's big furry paws tickled Kaa's back. Soon the python was giggling helplessly.

"Oooh, hee-hee-hee! That tickles! Stop! Ssstop! Get off, you big bag of fuzz!" Kaa sounded so funny Baloo started to laugh. When he reached the top of the pit, his tears were gone.

"I'm sure glad to be out of there," Baloo chuckled. "But what will we do with Kaa? We can't just leave him hanging."

"I know how to fix Kaa so he won't bother us for a while," Mowgli smiled. "Help me haul him up."

Together Baloo and Mowgli pulled Kaa up. Then, being very careful not to look at the SadStone himself, Mowgli held it in front of Kaa's eyes while he untied Kaa's tail.

"You're free now, Kaa," Mowgli said. But Kaa had forgotten all about Mowgli and Baloo. He was staring at the SadStone. First he sighed, then he sniffled. Then he burst into huge, scaly tears.

"Nobody undersssstands me," he cried. "All I want is a little sssqueeze now and then." As Mowgli and Baloo watched, Kaa slithered into the jungle, wailing loudly.

Mowgli tossed the SadStone back into the pit. "It belongs there where it can't make anyone else sad," he said. Then he and Baloo started home.

Bagheera met them on their way.

"Well?" he asked. "What happened?"

"You were right, Bagheera," Mowgli said. "It was pretty strange at that tower." He winked at Baloo. "But nothing happened worth crying about."

***Justin*, by Gavin A. Benjamin, 17, Brooklyn, New York**

YOUNG PHOTOGRAPHERS

The crumpled folds of a silk scarf . . . the dappled pattern of autumn leaves . . . a fiery ring of sunshine. With bold lines, soft shadows, and glowing colors, the young photographers whose works appear here show how they use their cameras creatively.

These photographs were among the winners in the photography division of the 1989 Scholastic Awards program. The contest is open to students in grades 7 through 12 at U.S. and Canadian schools. Entries are judged in two age divisions and three categories—color, black-and-white, and experimental (using unusual camera or darkroom techniques). The contest offers cash awards —and a chance for creative young people to earn the recognition they deserve.

Wrinkles & Yesterday,
by Jeannette Perry, 17,
Emporia, Kansas

Tree #1,
by Jeff Wilkinson, 17,
Brandon, Mississippi

Sparkling Sun,
by Kami Smith, 12,
Kingsport, Tennessee

The Architect,
by Kevin Swetnam, 14,
Bowie, Maryland

Personality,
by Mazana Bruggeman, 17,
Elmira, New York

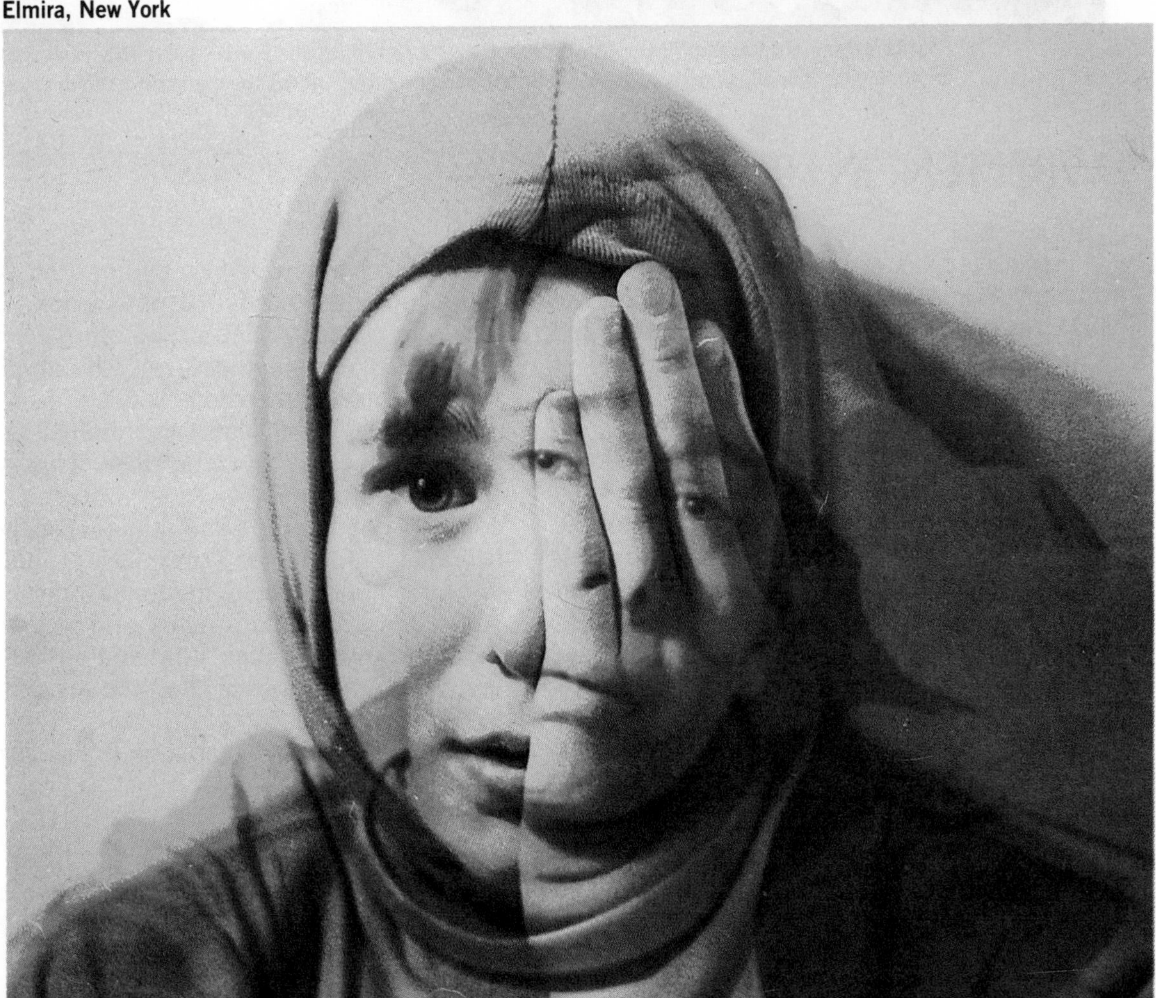

Fossils are ancient traces of living things, and they are records of the Earth's past. The fossil above is of an ammonite, a mollusk with a pearly shell that became extinct about the same time the dinosaurs did.

WRITTEN IN ROCK

Fossils are history written in rock. These ancient traces of living things—the delicate patterns of leaves and bones, the spirals and stars of vanished shellfish—are records of the Earth's past. They reveal the infinite variety and beauty of life.

A fossil may be just a sign left behind by some ancient animal—the impression of a dinosaur's foot or the remains of a primitive mammal's burrow. A fossil may be a shadowy mark left in rock by an ancient leaf that disappeared millions of years ago. Or a fossil may be the actual remains of a living thing, preserved forever in stone.

HOW FOSSILS FORM

Many fossils were formed by plants and animals that died and were quickly covered by silt, mud, clay, or perhaps the ash from a volcanic eruption. Over millions of years, the sediments hardened into rock. And, since they were sealed up before they had a chance to decay, these once-living things were preserved in various ways.

In some cases, plant and animal tissues became mineralized, or petrified. That is, the tissue changed to rock as water washed away its components and minerals seeped in to replace them. In other cases, minerals filled tiny air spaces in bones and shells, strengthening these tissues and preserving them through the ages. And sometimes minerals formed a mold around the outside of a shell or another hard structure. The shell eventually dissolved, leaving a perfect mold in the rock.

Some fossils are simply ghostly traces of things that once were. When a plant or animal decays, it may leave behind a deposit of carbon—a thin film that reveals its outline and structure. But some living things have been preserved nearly intact. Leaves and insects (and even some tiny vertebrates) have been found encased in amber, the fossilized resin of certain coniferous trees. Larger animals have been preserved for millions of years in deposits of tar and in the year-round ice of arctic regions.

Usually, however, only bits and pieces are found—a few bones or teeth, or fragments of plant leaves and stems. Hard tissues such as bones and shells, or the stems and veins of plants, are more likely to become fossils than soft tissues. This is because soft tissues decay quickly.

Whatever form a fossil takes, the process that leads to its creation can take thousands of years. And conditions must be exactly right. Thus, of all the billions of creatures that have lived on Earth, relatively few have left fossil remains. And many of those remains are buried in rock deep below the Earth's surface, where they may never be found.

Still, the Earth has changed greatly during its long history. Areas that once lay on the floor of ancient oceans have been pushed up to form mountains—and to reveal fossils. Fossils have been found on every continent, including Antarctica. Where they have been exposed to wind and rain, erosion has taken its toll and sometimes made the fossil record difficult to read. But people have been fascinated by fossils since early times.

FOSSIL THEORIES

When the ancient Greeks discovered the delicate forms of fossilized shells embedded in rocks, they correctly concluded that these fossils revealed the sites of ancient oceans. But other early theories about fossils weren't anywhere near as accurate. In the Middle Ages, some people believed that fossils were stones that fell to Earth during storms or lunar eclipses. Others thought that these lifelike forms actually developed inside rock, perhaps growing from tiny seeds.

The fossilized tusks of woolly mammoths were once thought to be unicorn horns. Certain fossils were also thought to have magical or medicinal powers—the ability to cure snakebite or the plague, for example. And

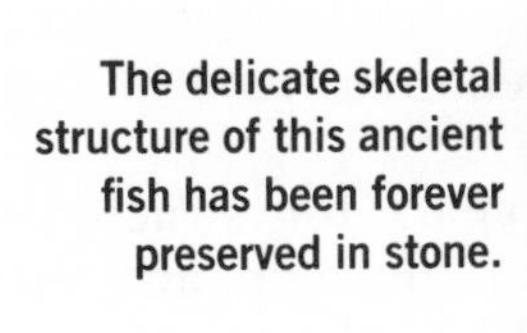

The delicate skeletal structure of this ancient fish has been forever preserved in stone.

American Indian legends held that the petrified trunks of ancient trees found in what is now Arizona were bones left from a battle between gods and giants.

Gradually, however, people began to reject such theories. Leonardo da Vinci, the Italian Renaissance scholar and artist, was among the first to realize that fossils were the remains of ancient animals that had been buried in sediment—sediment that had turned to stone.

It was many years before others adopted this view. But by the mid-1800's, many scientists accepted fossils as the remains of ancient life. And at about that time, Charles Darwin's work on the theory of evolution paved the way for the modern understanding of fossils.

Encased in rock, a 20-milion-year-old poplar leaf still retains the beautiful pattern of its veins.

READING THE RECORD

Fossil comes from a Latin word meaning "dug up." And scientists who study ancient life through fossils are called *paleontologists,* from Greek words meaning "existing long ago." These scientists date fossils by studying the rocks and other materials that encase them and by noting their place in the layers, or strata, of rock that have been laid down over the ages.

In the time scale that paleontologists use, even primitive mammals are newcomers—they appear in the fossil record less than 200 million years ago. The oldest fossils known are those of certain bacteria, one-celled organisms so simple that they lacked even a cell nucleus. These creatures lived almost 3.5 billion years ago.

It took millions of years for structures such as the cell nucleus to develop, and millions more for multi-celled plants and animals to appear. Some 600 million years ago, animals with shells and skeletons and plants with stems developed. At this point, the fossil record becomes truly rich, revealing how life proliferated first in the oceans and then on land.

Fossils have helped scientists piece together the story of evolution and discover how the forms of life we know developed from earlier forms. But there are still many gaps in the story—and many mysteries.

Among the mysteries are the many great extinctions that took place in the past. Over millions of years, countless strange and fantastic creatures have appeared, walked the Earth, and vanished. The most spectacular of these were the dinosaurs. These reptiles dominated all other life forms for 165 million years. But then, some 65 million years ago, they died out.

Dinosaurs weren't the only creatures to vanish. Ammonites were mollusks with pearly shells that developed long before the dinosaurs and died out at about the same time they did. Trilobites, distant relatives of today's spiders and crustaceans, were even more ancient. More than 10,000 species of these armor-plated ocean creatures developed before they disappeared some 230 million years ago. The fossil record doesn't explain why these and other creatures died out. It shows only that they once lived.

Still, fossils have revealed much about what life was like in ancient times. Scientists have found the fossilized nests, eggs, and young of dinosaurs. The fact that the young of some kinds of dinosaurs were more or less defenseless at birth indicates that their parents had to care for them. Thus we know that these dinosaurs, unlike most reptiles of today, were caring parents.

Fossils have also shown that some dinosaurs migrated in large herds and that, later in Earth's history, herds of camels and rhinoceroses roamed North America. And fossils have helped produce a picture of the ways in which the Earth's climate and land surfaces have changed.

Thanks to fossils, scientists know that frigid Antarctica once had a warm climate and that an inland sea once covered areas of the United States. Fossils have also helped scientists develop the theory of continental drift, which explains how the continents have moved to their present positions over millions of years. For example, fossils found in some of the older rock layers of South America are very similar to fossils found in India and southern Africa. This has led scientists to suppose that these land masses were once joined.

As scientists continue to search out fossils and study them, they will no doubt learn more secrets of the Earth's past. Through fossils, Earth's history is traced forever in stone.

FINDING FOSSILS

If you want to search for fossils, look first for an area where sedimentary rocks have been pushed up to the Earth's surface. These rocks, which include sandstone, shale, and limestone, were slowly built up in layers of fine particles. Most fossils are found in these rocks.

Sedimentary rocks can be found almost anywhere. But scientists who study fossils often make their richest finds near ancient bodies of water—in cliffs along dry streambeds or in areas that were once covered by the ocean, for example. This is because water speeds the process of mineralization by which many fossils form.

Fossil hunters may split open rocks in a search for traces of ancient plants or tiny animals. Or they may find fragments of fossilized teeth or bones. When such bits and pieces are found, the searchers comb the area for more fossils. The bones of a skeleton may be found together, relatively undisturbed. But more often, they are scattered. The workers may use heavy equipment to move large amounts of soil and rock at first. But around the delicate fossils (and especially around fragile fossilized bones) they use fine instruments to chip away rock and paintbrushes to clear away dust and soil.

When scientists find a fossil, they make careful records of its position and the layer of rock in which it was found. Then they usually move it—to a university, a museum, or some other site—for further study. To do this, they must strengthen and protect it. Cracks may be sealed with a gluelike substance that hardens to form a strong bond. Then the fossil may be encased in a cast, by wrapping it first in wet paper and then in burlap that has been soaked in plaster of paris.

If enough pieces are found, scientists are sometimes able to reconstruct the skeleton of an ancient animal. This allows them to picture what the animal actually looked like—even though it may not have walked the Earth for millions of years.

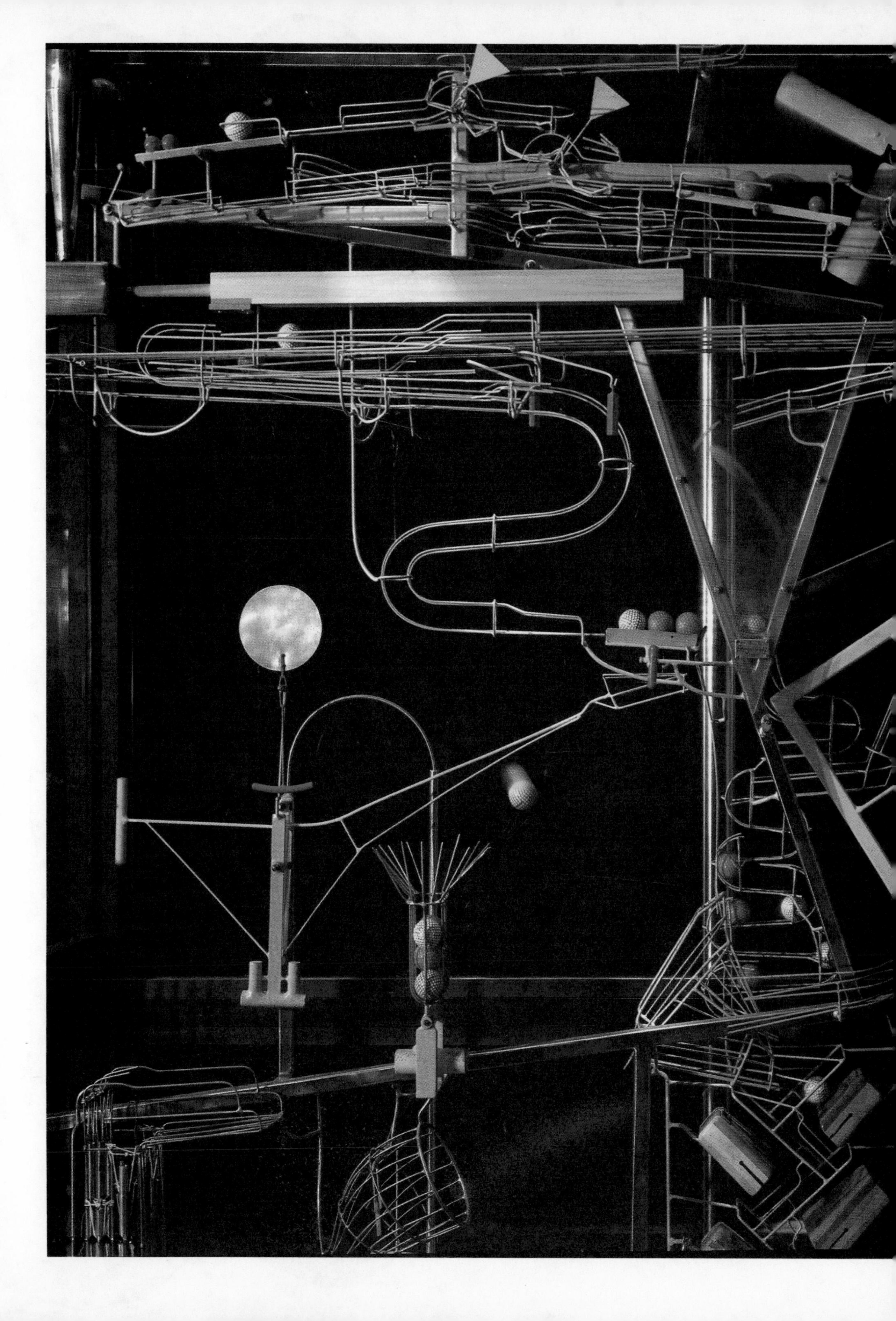

GREAT GIZMOS

It whirs, clunks, clatters, and chimes. Wheels spin, pendulums swing, and balls roll and bounce all over the place. This fascinating gizmo is a sculpture by the U.S. artist George Rhoads. Called *Having a Ball,* it's one of several similar works that the artist has created for all sorts of public places.

Rhoads' works are called *audiokinetic* sculptures, from Greek words meaning "sound" and "motion." And while each sculpture is different, sound and motion are central to all of them. In these works, balls are released at random onto various tracks. They travel down ramps, stairways, spirals, and loop-the-loops. They may drop onto a tiny trampoline and bounce up into a basket. Several may collect in a dumper and then be released all at once, in a flurry of activity.

Along the way, the balls set wheels and pendulums in motion and strike chimes, bells, and other noisemaking devices. At the end of the trip, they usually fall into a large metal bowl, producing a resonant, ringing noise as they spiral to the bottom. There they exit through a hole and are carried by a motorized chain back to the top of the sculpture, to begin the journey again.

The sculptures use basic mechanical principles, and many of the parts are everyday items. (The bowl that catches the balls at the end, for example, is often a wok, a Chinese cooking pot.) And apart from the chain motor, all the activity of each sculpture is produced by gravity.

Rhoads' works have been set up in airports and shopping centers, as well as in the Boston Museum of Science and other museums. One of the largest, *Ball City,* stands 24 feet (8 meters) tall in Canada's West Edmonton Mall. Another, *42nd Street Ballroom,* is in the main bus terminal in New York City.

Wherever these sculptures are, people watch in trancelike fascination. Part of the attraction is the appeal of seeing mechanical things work. Part is the puzzle of the intricate patterns of sound and motion produced by the balls. But the works also have a whimsical air. Watching them, it's hard not to think that the balls are having fun as they bounce and clatter along.

VOYAGE TO OUTER SPACE

In August, 1989, the U.S. spacecraft Voyager 2 became the first visitor to the planet Neptune from Earth. As the unmanned spacecraft passed within 3,000 miles (4,800 kilometers) of Neptune, it beamed back pictures of a cold blue world with eight moons —one of them pink.

Voyager had been launched in 1977 to explore the outer reaches of the solar system. It had traveled 4.4 billion miles (7.1 billion kilometers) to reach Neptune. On the way, it had flown by Jupiter in 1979, Saturn in 1981, and Uranus in 1986, sending back vast amounts of information. And in 1989 it discovered much about Neptune.

Neptune is so far away that Voyager's radio signals took four hours to reach Earth. Computers turned the faint signals into bright pictures, and Neptune appeared as a pale blue planet. Its atmosphere was filled with white clouds and swirling storms. An enormous dark area called the Great Dark Spot turned out to be a hurricane-like storm the size of Earth. One scientist said that it reminded him of a "big piece of pizza dough rotating round and round."

Voyager found a system of rings circling Neptune, like the rings around Saturn. There are three major rings, with fields of dust in between. And the spacecraft counted eight moons. Only two of the moons—Triton and Nereid—had been known before. The six newly discovered moons are small and irregular in shape, with very dark surfaces.

Triton is Neptune's largest moon, and its surface has a pinkish color. It is the only moon in the solar system known to orbit its planet in a direction opposite the planet's direction of rotation. Triton has its own atmosphere. And it is the coldest place known in the solar system, with surface temperatures of about −370°F (−220°C). Voyager also found evidence of volcanoes on Triton. The only other objects in the solar system known to have active volcanoes are Earth and Jupiter's moon Io.

As Voyager left Neptune, it headed out of the solar system. It carried a gold-plated disc of sounds and images from Earth. If creatures from other worlds should ever intercept Voyager, they will find greetings recorded in 55 languages, pictures of nature, and music by composers ranging from Beethoven to Chuck Berry.

In August, Voyager 2 became the first spacecraft to visit Neptune—the pale blue planet. Circling the planet is a hurricane-like storm the size of Earth, called the Great Dark Spot.

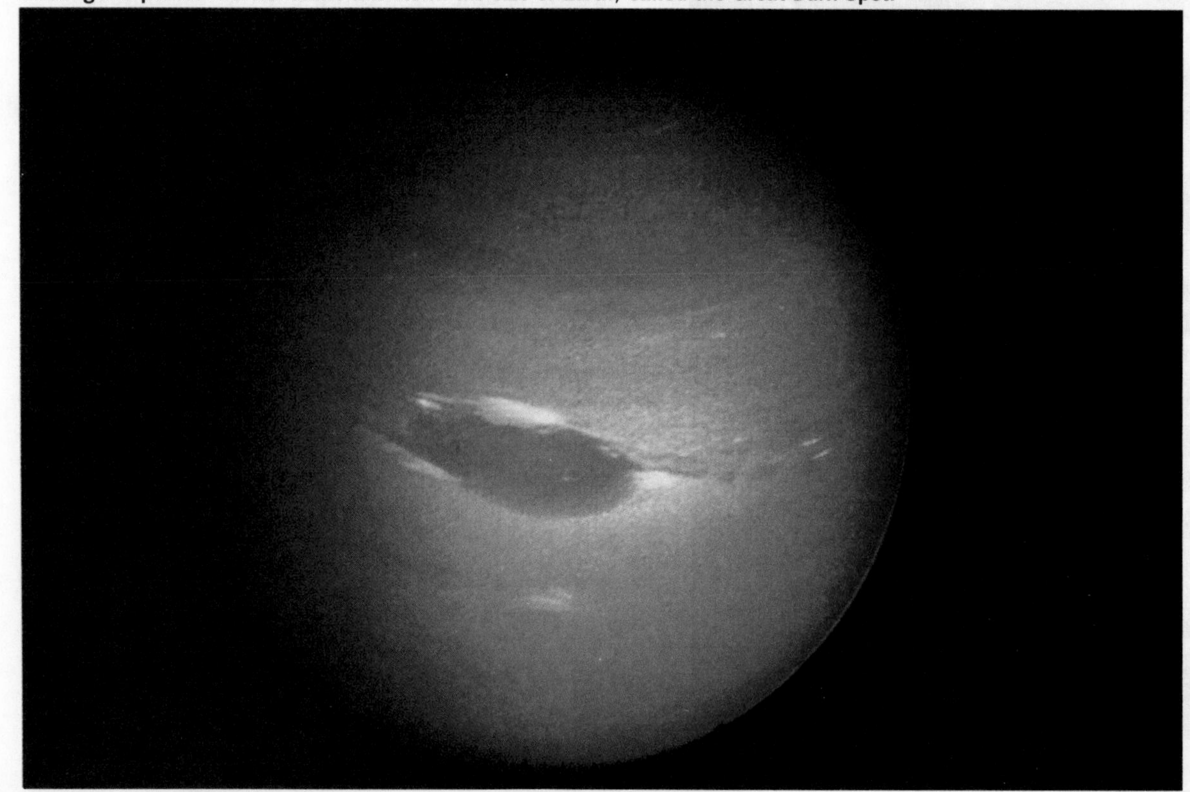

PENCIL PALS

Do you ever have days where everything seems to go wrong? Well, just make friends with a pencil pal, and you can let the world know if you're having a good day or a bad one!

Your pal is made by gluing a piece of long-haired fake fur around the top of a pencil. Add some goo-goo eyes, a pom-pom nose, and a bow. When you're in a happy frame of mind, your pal will look sleek and content. But when you're upset, just whirl the pencil between the palms of your hands so that your pal's ''hair'' goes flying in every direction—reflecting your frazzled mood.

Your pal may even help cheer you up by getting you to smile—great medicine for anyone who is feeling down.

THE NEW ZOO

You move quietly down the forest path until, peering through the tropical foliage, you see them—a troop of gorillas on a grassy knoll. Just in front of you, a female gorilla sits cuddling her baby in her arms. Suddenly the mother senses your presence. With a snort, she knuckle-walks out of sight behind the knoll, her baby clinging tightly to her back.

You might think you're in Africa. But in fact, you're in Atlanta, Georgia—at the Atlanta Zoo. The gorilla exhibit there (shown in the photo above) is typical of a new trend. Where zoos once took animals from the wild and locked them in prisonlike cages, they now re-create entire habitats—the tropical rain forest, the polar ice pack, the plains of Africa. The animals can roam contentedly in natural surroundings.

This new look reflects a new concern at zoos: conservation. All over the world, animal homes are disappearing. People cut down or burn forests to plant crops and build new homes. Pollution poisons the air and water. And as people make deeper inroads into natural habitats, more and more animal species are in danger of dying out.

Governments, wildlife and conservation groups, and concerned people everywhere are working to halt this destruction. And in recent years, zoos have become leaders in the fight. The new exhibits are part of their effort. Besides making the animals happier, these exhibits teach people about the importance of natural habitats. They allow scientists to study natural animal behavior. And because the animals are more relaxed in these settings, they are more likely to breed and reproduce. Thus zoos have begun to help keep rare and endangered species alive.

THE NEW LOOK

Most of the new zoo exhibits combine natural and artificial materials to simulate animal habitats. They may spread over acres of land, or they may be enclosed in buildings where the exact climate conditions of the habitat can be reproduced. Bars, walls, and fences are kept to a minimum. Instead, glass and natural barriers—rocks, streams, cliffs, moats, and the like—are used wherever possible to separate people from animals (and to separate predatory animals from the others).

Here are some examples:

• Ten minutes from downtown Seattle, Washington, the Woodland Park Zoo is designed as a series of open habitats from different parts of the world. The zoo's latest addition is an Asian tropical forest. The first section of this exhibit—Elephant Forest—opened in 1989 with a meandering stream, waterfalls, a bathing pool, and a Thai-style elephant barn. For the future, the zoo plans indoor and outdoor habitats for tigers, siamangs, orangutans, and other creatures of tropical Asia.

• Near Chicago, Illinois, the Brookfield Zoo has re-created rain forests from three regions—South America, Africa, and Asia—in one of the largest zoo buildings ever constructed. Inside, there are towering jungle trees, dangling vines, and rushing waterfalls. As realistic as the scenes appear, many features are artificial—cliffs and rocks are made of gunite (a type of concrete), and many plants are made of metal and epoxy. The temperature averages 78°F (25°C) year-round, and there are thunderstorms at least three times a day.

In this tropical environment, animals that once lived in cages roam freely. From South America are golden lion tamarins and other monkeys, a two-toed sloth, a tapir, a giant anteater, and many birds. From Asia are orangutans, macaques, and other monkeys, along with small-clawed otters and birds such as the magpie robin and fairy bluebird. From Africa are more birds and monkeys, gorillas, and a pygmy hippo.

• In Texas, the Dallas Zoo is developing an exhibit called the Wilds of Africa that will reproduce the major habitats of that continent. The exhibit is scheduled to open in 1990 and will cover 25 acres. Visitors will ride a monorail or walk down trails through replicas of an African desert, bush, forest, river, and mountainside. In the forest, more than 30 kinds of birds will fly overhead, and monkeys will chatter in the trees. Herons and waterbuck will wade in the river. A special observation post will allow visitors to spy on the animals of the bush. A highlight of the exhibit will be a two-acre gorilla habitat. Visitors will watch them from an underground bunker or from a thatched-roofed field research station, where scientists will study the behavior of these magnificent animals.

• In Indianapolis, Indiana, officials took a hard look at their old zoo, with its cages and fences, and decided to build a completely new facility. The new zoo opened in 1988 and has three times as much space as the old one. More than 2,000 animals live in simulated habitats that reproduce the deserts, plains, forests, and waters of the world. Special features include a re-creation of the Amazon jungle; a desert conservatory where plants, lizards, and venomous snakes can be seen; and natural settings for Siberian tigers, Kodiak bears, and Japanese macaques.

The Woodland Park Zoo in Seattle is designed as a series of open habitats. The newest exhibit is the Elephant Forest, with a stream, waterfalls, and a bathing pool.

• The Cincinnati Zoo is one of the oldest zoos in the United States, but it has been at the forefront of new zoo trends. This zoo has exhibited animals in natural settings since the 1930's, when the idea was first introduced. Recently, many older exhibits have been renovated, and new ones have been added. The zoo now features a Cat House where visitors can look through glass panels at sixteen different cat species, each in a re-created natural habitat. Another exhibit, Big Cat Canyon, is home to a group of white Bengal tigers. The red panda exhibit features plants that are found in these animals' Chinese homeland. The zoo has also added a large collection of insects, from goliath beetles to Madagascar hissing cockroaches.

• An even older zoo, the tiny Central Park Zoo in New York City, re-opened in 1988 after a $35 million renovation. On just 5½ acres, this new zoo now presents three climate zones: the polar regions, where penguins and polar bears frolic; the temperate zone; and the tropics, complete with exotic birds, snakes, and monkeys.

• The San Diego Zoo, in Southern California, pioneered in developing natural exhibits where visitors are separated from animals only by moats and similar barriers. Now the zoo has begun to create complete habitats: One of its newest additions is Tiger River, a three-acre canyon filled with a tropical rain forest. A computerized irrigation and fogging system provides the humidity required by the jungle plants in the forest. As visitors walk through Tiger River's ten exhibits, they see crocodiles, Chinese water dragons, web-footed fishing cats, tapirs, pythons, and dozens of birds. The feature attraction is a group of Sumatran tigers (one of the smallest and rarest species), which can be seen lounging in the grass and splashing in pools.

At the Cincinnati Zoo's new Cat House, visitors can look through glass panels at different cat species, such as this clouded leopard cub. Each species is in a replica of its natural habitat.

• Many other zoos are also developing natural exhibits. Not all depict exotic habitats like tropical rain forests and the African bush—some show threatened habitats closer to home. The Audubon Zoo, in New Orleans, Louisiana, has reproduced a section of a Louisiana swamp, complete with alligators (even some white ones). The Arizona-Sonora Desert Museum, in Tucson, Arizona, has desert mountain habitats where black bears, mountain lions, and Mexican gray wolves can be seen.

In St.-Félicien, Canada (north of Quebec City), the St.-Félicien Zoo has developed a similar area for Canadian wildlife. Here, in a park that covers more than 950 acres, some 40 different species of native Canadian animals roam freely. Only the wolves are behind bars. Visitors ride through the park in special cars protected by metal grilles—so that the people, rather than the animals, are caged. The park re-creates Canada's three main habitats: the prairie, the taiga, and the tundra. Each is given its characteristic plants and animals—black bear, moose, caribou, bison, and musk ox among them.

NEW CONCERNS

The new zoo exhibits are popular with visitors, who get to see animals as they appear in the wild. But zoo officials say that this is only part of the reason they are placing their animals in more natural surroundings. When animals live more naturally, they can be studied to learn how they behave in the wild. This information may help conservationists save species that are threatened.

Zoos are helping to save wild animals in other ways, too. With computers and other high-tech equipment, zoo scientists are learning more about animal nutrition. This information, too, may help endangered species survive. And most major zoos now have extensive education programs, designed to make people more aware of the plight of wildlife worldwide.

Perhaps the most ambitious zoo programs are those that attempt to breed rare animals. A number of zoos have had success with animals ranging from antelopes to Siberian tigers. The San Diego Zoo is involved in a project to breed California condors. Along with the San Diego Wild Animal Park and the Los Angeles Zoo, it is caring for the last living representatives of this species. The Cincinnati Zoo is conducting research in animal reproduction. The Washington Park Zoo in Portland, Oregon, and Busch Gardens in Tampa, Florida, are raising rare Asian elephants.

Special reserves have also been set up by some zoos. At these centers, which are away from the zoos and aren't open to the public, the animals can roam freely and breed. The National Zoo, in Washington, D.C., has a conservation and research center in Virginia. And New York City's Bronx Zoo has a reserve on an island off Georgia.

When zoos breed animals, they no longer have to take them from the wild. And in many cases, the goal of these breeding programs isn't simply to produce more animals for zoos. The idea is to release animals back into the wild. In this way, people can help undo some of the damage that has been done to wild animal species.

Of course, even when zoo animals are in natural settings, they are still captive. Some people are critical of zoos for this reason. Instead of spending money on elaborate exhibits, they say, it would be better to help endangered species in the wild. And they point out that in many zoos, the animals still live in poor conditions.

Supporters of the new programs answer that zoos are playing an important role in conservation just by helping people learn more about animals. And if natural habitats continue to be destroyed, zoos may become the last refuge for threatened species.

One of the newest additions at the San Diego Zoo is Tiger River, a three-acre canyon filled with a tropical rain forest. A computerized irrigation and fogging system provides the humidity needed by the jungle plants.

WILDLIFE NEEDS YOU!

Wildlife conservation is a new concern for zoos all over the world. Many zoos are finding new ways to make people more aware of the plight of endangered species and threatened natural habitats. And in California, the San Diego Zoo has developed an imaginative way to promote concern for wildlife: an annual art contest.

Each year, artists of all kinds—young and old, amateur and professional—are invited to submit works based on a theme chosen by the zoo. The idea has proved to be very popular: In its first year alone, 1988, the contest drew more than 1,300 entries on the theme "Wildlife Needs You." The two works shown here were among the first-place winners. (The top picture, by Yvette Hoyt, won in the category for grades 7 to 9; the one at the right, by Anne Reas, won in the category for grades 10 to 12.) Winning works were displayed at the zoo. And two works were chosen to be reproduced on San Diego Zoo posters.

The Sorcerer's Apprentice

The great sorcerer paced around his cavern. It had been a dull day. Even creating his favorite magical spells hadn't been fun.

He watched his young apprentice, Mickey, trudge back again from the fountain in the courtyard with buckets of water to fill the huge cistern in the cave. It might be fun to turn Mickey into something, he thought. But then the apprentice couldn't finish his work. Instead, the sorcerer conjured up a huge bat.

Mickey stopped to watch as the bat became a beautiful green butterfly, and then disappeared in a shower of sparkles. He wished he could perform such dazzling feats. But his master wouldn't let him try.

The sorcerer was still bored. Leaving his hat on the table, he went out.

Mickey watched his master go. "It's not fair," he thought. "I've been with Yen Sid for a long time, and all I do is chop wood, stir potions, scrub floors, and carry water. I want to make magic, too."

He sighed. He had been carrying water up and down the stairs all morning, and the cistern was only half full.

Mickey looked at Yen Sid's tall, pointed hat. That hat had great powers.

"Here's my chance!" Mickey thought. "I'll use the hat and cast a spell or two!"

His hands trembled with excitement as he put the hat on and waited for something terrible to happen. Nothing did.

Mickey danced about the cave. He noticed an old broom leaning against the wall. And he had a grand idea.

Rolling up his sleeves, he tried to remember what Yen Sid did. He stared at the broom and drew back his arms and waved them hard. The broom didn't move. He wiggled his fingers. The broom stood still.

"All right," thought Mickey. "Here comes a double whammy!" He tried again with a mighty, sweeping gesture!

The broom began to glow. It started to quiver. Mickey waved again and again.

The broom twitched and stood up. Mickey was amazed. He had made the broom come to life! Why, he was every bit as great a sorcerer as Yen Sid!

Mickey didn't want to stop. He told the broom to walk, so the broomstraws separated into two fat feet. The broom took a few wobbly steps.

Mickey's plan was working. He gave his next command, and two thick arms with strong hands popped out from the broom handle. Delighted with his new powers, Mickey ordered the broom to follow him to the cistern.

Beside it were the two heavy wooden water buckets. Mickey motioned for the broom to pick them up. The broom obeyed, and Mickey smiled. His magic was working.

Gleefully, he led the broom across the chamber, up the stairs, and into the courtyard to the fountain. Then he pointed.

Obediently, the broom filled the buckets and then followed Mickey downstairs to the cistern. At Mickey's signal, the broom poured the water into the huge vat.

Back and forth from the fountain to the cistern Mickey skipped, with the broom tagging along. When Mickey was sure the broom knew what to do, he plopped down in the sorcerer's chair.

"Now, this is what an apprentice's life should be," he told himself. "Why work, if I can use magic to do my chores?" As the broom trotted back and forth with buckets of water, Mickey closed his eyes to dream about what magic spells he could cast next.

"I could do anything I want," he thought dreamily. "Why, I could float right up to the stars!"

Suddenly, Mickey was drifting skyward. He saw stars winking merrily at him, and he winked back. His feet touched something hard. He realized he was standing on top of a high, steep cliff. In the sky a line of planets whirled past. More planets swept by in the other direction. A comet flashed far off in space. Mickey beckoned to it, and it swooped toward him.

At Mickey's command, the comet sped away, crashing into the planets and showering the sky with sparkling fragments.

Mickey watched the fragments fall into a pounding ocean at the base of the cliff.

"I'll command the waves to go higher!" Mickey thought. He waved his right arm. A huge wave broke against the cliff. He motioned with his left arm. Crash! Another big wave broke, spraying the air with foam.

Mickey was thrilled! He swooped his arm to the right, then to the left, again and again. Each time, the waves came higher and closer. Suddenly a mighty wave splashed Mickey, drenching him from head to foot.

He shivered—and woke up!

"Where am I?" Mickey wondered. The cliff and ocean were gone. But there was water everywhere!

While Mickey had been dreaming, the broom had been working. Now the cistern was overflowing.

"I've got to stop the broom!" Mickey realized. He tugged on it. But the broom kept marching. Mickey lunged for it, and tripped and tumbled into the water as the broom disappeared outside.

Gasping and spluttering, Mickey rushed upstairs to stop the broom. But it just brushed past him. As Mickey clung to a bucket, the broom dragged him through the water and tossed him into the cistern, too!

Scrambling out, Mickey shouted magic words to break the spell. "Abracadabra! Alakazoola! Famitz and grimble!" he cried. That didn't work.

Frantically, Mickey looked around for something to stop the broom. He saw an ax and grabbed it. He ran outside to the fountain where the broom stood and raised the ax. Chop! Chop! In seconds, the broom was a pile of splinters.

It was suddenly very quiet. Mickey walked into the cave and shut the door. Then he heard a strange noise from the courtyard. Hardly daring to breathe, he peeked outside.

"Oh, no!" Mickey was horrified. Every splinter had become a broom. Every broom had two buckets! And they were all marching his way. Mickey slammed the door and leaned against it, but the brooms pushed it open and knocked him down. Broom after broom tramped over him, down the stairs.

The water rose higher and higher. But the brooms went on, through the water, under the water, emptying bucket after bucket of water into the overflowing cistern.

Stools, chairs and tables floated by. A spare bucket went past. Mickey grabbed it and tried to bail, but there was nowhere to throw the water.

A big book of magic drifted by. Mickey scrambled onto it and turned its pages, looking for a spell—any spell—to stop the brooms. But he couldn't read the strange words.

Mickey clung to the book as the water whirled him around in circles. The brooms kept marching. All seemed lost. And then . . .

There stood Yen Sid, at the top of the stairs, gazing at the wild scene below. Slowly, silently he descended.

Mickey clutched the magic book and stared as the sorcerer approached. Would he walk right into the water?

But with each step Yen Sid took, the water pulled back. Then, with a mighty gesture, Yen Sid raised his arms, Instantly, the water disappeared, dumping Mickey onto the floor.

He sat up and rubbed his eyes. The floor was dry. Every drop of water was gone. And everything was back in its place.

Mickey looked sheepishly at the sorcerer. Then he got up and walked slowly toward his master. Yen Sid said nothing. Looking and feeling very ashamed, Mickey took off the sorcerer's hat and handed it to him. Still, the sorcerer was silent.

What was Yen Sid going to do? Would he turn Mickey into a fish, or a frog? Nervously, Mickey handed the broom to his master. Then he picked up his buckets and crept quietly toward the door, with the hairs on the back of his neck prickling in fear.

Yen Sid raised the broom. He aimed it at Mickey. Then—WHACK! He smacked Mickey in the seat. Mickey leaped into the air and flew out the door.

As Yen Sid watched Mickey go, he smiled a little. His apprentice had learned an important lesson. And as for himself, he certainly wasn't bored anymore!

BODY TRICKS

Do you want to impress your friends? Then play a few body tricks on them and watch their amazement. With a little knowledge of the human body and how it works, you can make your friends believe that you are performing magic!

LEVITATING ARMS

By tricking a friend's nervous system, you can make him believe that his arms are levitating, or rising, at your command.

Ask your friend to stand in a doorway and push the backs of his hands against the sides of the door frame. Tell him to press as hard as possible against the door frame while you count to 25. Then have your friend step quickly out of the doorway. As your friend moves forward, say: "Oh arms, I command you to rise." Your friend's arms will slowly rise in the air.

Why does this happen? Your friend's brain had been sending messages to the muscles of his arms, telling them to press against the door frame. For a moment after your friend steps out of the doorway, his muscles are still receiving these messages. And with nothing to press against, his arms will levitate.

SUPER FINGERS

Show one of your strongest friends that just two of your fingers can be more powerful than her clenched fists.

Ask your friend to clench her fists and place one fist on top of the other, with her arms straight out in front. Predict that no matter how hard she presses her fists together, you can separate them with just two of your fingers.

Now take your two index fingers and place one on either side of her fists; using these fingers, knock her fists sideways in opposite directions. Do this very quickly.

This trick works because your friend is thinking of one action while you are planning to do something else. She's applying force in an up-and-down direction and isn't ready for the unexpected force that you apply from the sides.

STICKY FINGERS

Tell your friend that you know a magic spell that will ''cement'' two of his fingers together.

Ask your friend to form a steeple with his index fingers while pressing the knuckles of his other fingers together. Ask him to separate the two index fingers—this will be easy to do. Have him start again, this time using his middle fingers to form the steeple. It will be more difficult for him to separate the middle fingers, but it will still be possible. Finally, ask your friend to form the steeple with his ring fingers. Now place your magic spell . . . as long as his knuckles are pressed together, your friend will be unable to separate his ring fingers!

This trick works because some muscles in a person's body are stronger than other muscles. The muscles in the ring fingers are weaker than the muscles that keep the knuckles pressed together.

MAGIC WEIGHT

One minute two friends can lift you off the ground; the next it's impossible!

First, place your hands securely on your shoulders with your elbows pointing toward the floor. Ask two friends to stand on either side of you and lift you up by your elbows. They should be able to do so easily.

Now ask your friends if they think they will be able to lift you by the elbows if you keep your hands on your shoulders but move your arms to a different position. They will probably say "yes."

Once again place your hands securely on your shoulders. But this time hold your arms so that your elbows are pointing straight out in front of you. In this position, your friends will find it impossible to lift you by your elbows.

When you move your arms, you move the elbows away from your center of gravity (the point at which your body weight is centered). The farther away your elbows are from your center of gravity, the harder it is for your friends to lift you straight up.

STICKY CHAIRS

Here's a trick that's certain to keep your friends "glued" to their chairs.

Ask a friend to sit in a chair with his back straight, his head back, and his chin tipped up. Tell him that no matter how strong he is, you can keep him in his seat using only the tip of one finger.

Now place your index finger on his forehead and, pressing firmly, tell him to stand up. He won't be able to move!

This trick, too, depends on the way your friend's body is centered. When he sits in the chair, his center of gravity is over the chair seat. To stand up, he must lean forward so that his weight is over his feet. And the pressure of your finger is all it takes to keep him from doing this.

POWER PLAY

This is a good trick to play on a friend who thinks he's stronger than you. Challenge him to raise your hand up off your head. Sound simple?

Tell your friend to stand next to you and keep both feet on the ground. Now place your hand firmly on your head, with your forearm in a horizontal position. Tell your friend to lift your hand from your head. No matter how hard he tries, he won't be able to do it.

Only someone much taller than you might be successful in raising your hand. Why does your friend fail? Because he is actually trying to lift the weight of your entire body. And as long as he remains at your side with both feet on the ground, he's in the wrong position to lift you.

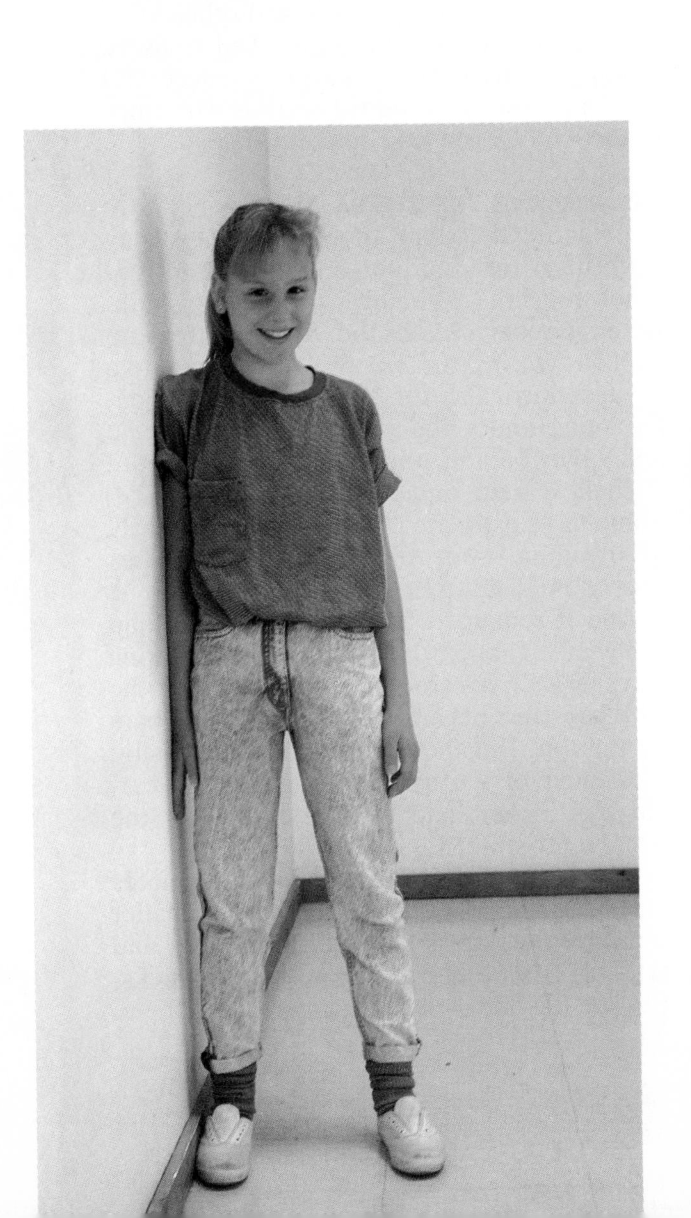

FALLING FEET

The next time a friend brags about her gymnastic skills, ask her if she can balance on one foot. "Of course!" she will reply, and probably demonstrate how easy it is to do. But, you ask, can she do this anywhere in the room? "Of course," she'll again reply. But you can prove her wrong! Tell her there's a certain spot in the room where it will be impossible to balance on one leg.

Have your friend stand next to a wall. She should be as close to the wall as possible. Her arm should lie flat against the wall, and the outside of her foot should touch the bottom of the wall. Now ask her to lift her outside foot and keep her balance. She won't be able to do this. It's impossible!

Why? To stand on one foot, your friend has to be able to shift all her weight onto the other foot. The wall prevents her from doing this.

LOST TREASURE

On a quiet, moonlit night in the 1600's, a band of pirates works feverishly to finish digging a deep shaft on a barren, windswept island. For days, these bandits of the sea have been tunneling deep down into the bowels of the tiny island. Now, their bodies covered with mist and sweat, they have completed their work. The shaft—nearly 200 feet (60 meters) deep, with side tunnels branching out like limbs from a tree trunk—is finished. They have created a "pirate bank," into which they can "deposit" the loot they have plundered from unlucky merchant ships.

Pirate treasure! Half a billion dollars worth—possibly much more—may now lie at the bottom of that shaft on Oak Island, which is in the Atlantic Ocean off the coast of Nova Scotia, Canada. Many people think the shaft is the hiding place for the booty taken by such notorious pirates as William Kidd and Henry Morgan. But no one is really sure. And for nearly 200 years, treasure hunters have been trying to solve the riddle of Oak Island. Millions of dollars have been spent, and six people have lost their lives, trying to get to the bottom of the mysterious shaft.

Oak Island isn't the only place that has lured treasure hunters. In every age, and in all parts of the world, there have been people who have spent fortunes and risked their lives in the hope of finding fabulous wealth. Why are people willing to risk so much on what is often a fool's errand?

Almost everyone dreams of getting rich without doing much work. And treasure hunting has the added appeal of romantic adventure. In the popular image, a treasure hunter is a swashbuckling figure with a gun in one hand and a treasure map in the other. Think of the cunning pirate Long John Silver in Robert Louis Stevenson's adventure novel *Treasure Island,* or Indiana Jones in the action-packed film *Raiders of the Lost Ark*.

In reality, today's treasure seekers are more likely to rely on sonar and other high-tech tools than on old maps. And treasure hunting is hard work—even a successful search can be long and frustrating. The story of the *Atocha* is a case in point.

THE WRECK OF THE ATOCHA

At about the same time that pirates may have been burying loot on Oak Island, another treasure was being lost far to the south. In September, 1622, the Spanish treasure galleon *Nuestra Señora de Atocha* ran into a savage hurricane off the coast of Florida. Groaning under the weight of tons of gold and silver bullion, the *Atocha* smashed into a shallow reef and sank without a trace. Some have estimated its rich cargo at nearly $400 million—one of the richest treasures ever to be lost at sea.

And it remained lost, too, for more than 350 years. Then, in 1985, a group of seafaring salvagers discovered the main hull of the *Atocha*—and began bringing up silver bars by the ton. But the find hadn't come easily; the leader of the treasure hunters, 64-year-old Mel Fisher, had been searching for the *Atocha* for sixteen years.

Over the years, Fisher and his associates had been successful in dredging up smaller treasures, mostly silver and gold coins and artifacts from other old Spanish shipwrecks. But the big find—the *Atocha*—eluded them.

Then Fisher hired a scholar to comb through more than 50,000 pages of dusty old documents in the Spanish archives. One document was a report by Spanish salvagers sent to locate the *Atocha* shortly after it went down. The report pinpointed the wreck's location as about 40 miles (65 kilometers) from Key West, Florida.

In his hunt for the *Atocha,* Fisher equipped his salvage boat with sensitive metal detectors and the most modern sonar devices, to produce charts of the ocean floor. And he placed pipes over the propeller to drive jets of clear water down, clearing away silt at the murky bottom so that divers could spot objects of interest.

Even with all this technology, it took Fisher and his divers many years to locate the *Atocha*. But in the end patience paid off. On July 20, 1985, he and his crew members hit the jackpot. Divers bobbed to the surface of the Atlantic shouting, "We found it!" What they had found, as one member of the group put it, was "a reef of silver bars with lobsters living in it."

Crew members and investors will have a tidy sum to share when the final haul is totaled up. And archeologists and historians

Over the years, divers have dredged up small treasures (*left*) from some of the many sunken ships lying beneath the seas. But the discovery of the *Atocha* yielded a "gold mine" of treasures, among them the fabulous gold chains below.

The Oak Island Mystery: Is the Money Pit actually a pirate bank into which pirates "deposited" the loot they plundered from unlucky merchant ships? Treasure hunters have been trying to find out for nearly 200 years.

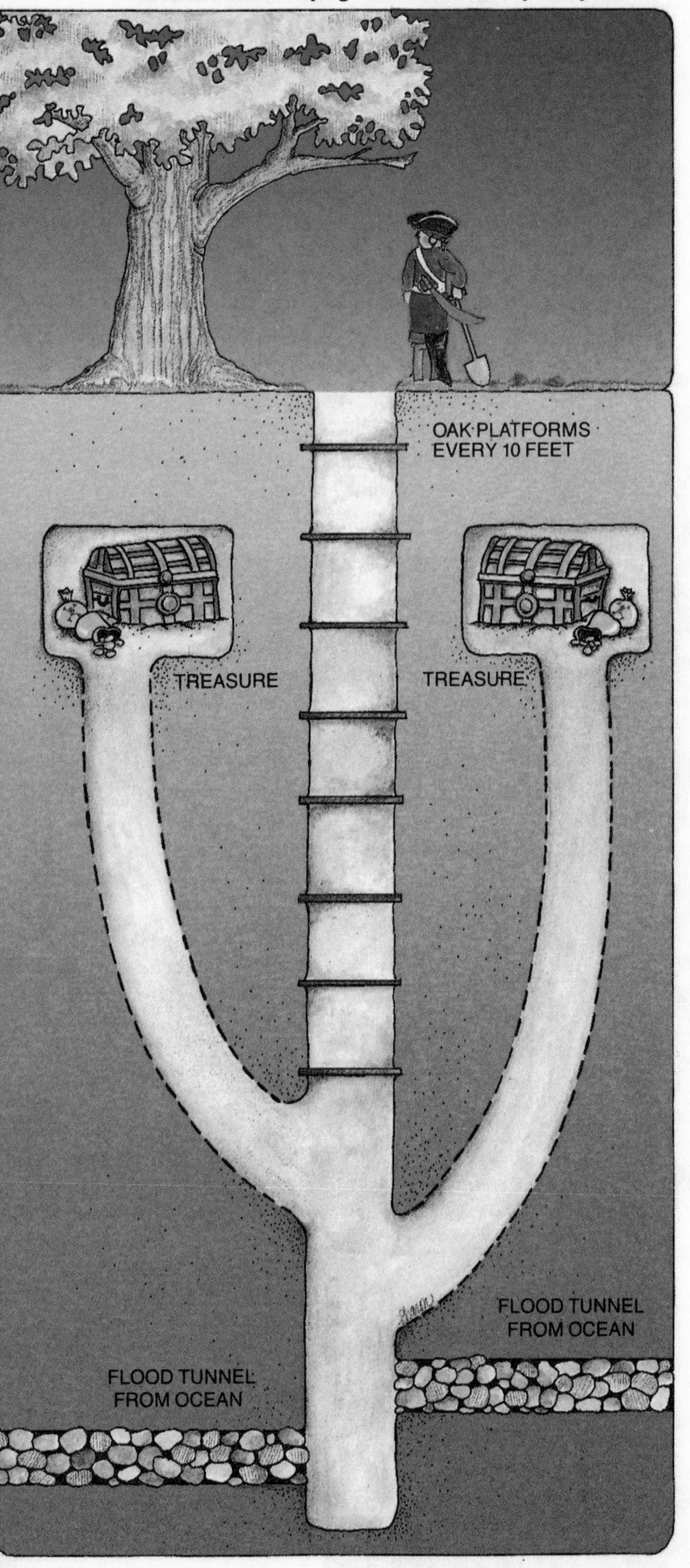

will learn more about the past from the tools, crockery, and pieces of hull brought up from the wreck site.

MORE MISSING MILLIONS

The *Atocha* is only one of an estimated 2,000 wrecks lying beneath the Atlantic Ocean and the Caribbean Sea. Billions of dollars worth of gold, silver, and precious gems were taken from the Indians of Mexico and South America by the Spanish. But many Spanish ships—and later ships, too—ran afoul of treacherous reefs or were ripped apart by gale-force winds. In fact, in 1989 salvagers located a nearly intact Spanish galleon off the Florida coast. And another group of treasure hunters began bringing up wealth from one of the richest wrecks ever: the paddle-wheel steamer *Central America*. This ship was bound for New York when it sank off South Carolina in 1857. On board were three tons of gold and the personal fortunes of passengers who had struck it rich in the California Gold Rush.

Perhaps by now you're eager to go treasure hunting. Where do you look? Let's take a quick tour of some of the places where vast treasures may still be found.

- **Colombia's Lake of Gold.** For centuries, the Muisca Indians of Colombia heaped piles of gold and jewels at the feet of each newly crowned chief, in a ceremony at the lake of Guatavita. As an offering to the gods, the chief would throw the entire fortune into the lake. Generations of fortune hunters have tried various techniques, even trying to drain the lake, to retrieve the treasure. But only a few golden objects have been found.
- **The Lost Dutchman Mine.** In the rugged Superstition Mountains of Arizona sits what may be one of the world's richest gold mines. A Mexican named Miguel Peralta was the first person known to have struck it rich there. A few decades later, a German gold seeker named Jacob "the Dutchman" Waltz rediscovered the mine. Waltz died in 1891, but he is supposed to have left behind a map showing the mine's location.

Maybe you'll be the lucky—or unlucky—one to find the lost mine. Just remember that nearly everyone who has stumbled upon the mine has met an untimely end. Some were murdered. Others died of the desert heat or the venomous bites of rattlesnakes.

• **The Real Treasure Island.** Some 300 miles (485 kilometers) off the Pacific coast of Costa Rica lies Cocos Island, which many believe served as inspiration for Robert Louis Stevenson's novel *Treasure Island.* Cocos was a waystation for the pirate chiefs who were the scourge of the seas in the days of the Spanish Empire. A half dozen pirate treasures are believed to be buried there. And a hoard of wealth taken out of Peru by Spanish nobles in the 1820's is believed to be hidden in a cave on Cocos.

All this wealth has been a magnet for some 450 separate treasure-hunting expeditions. So far no one has made a big find, despite a century of blasting and digging. And now the Costa Rican government has declared the island off limits to treasure hunters because of damage to plants and animals.

• **The Oak Island Mystery.** The most fascinating unsolved treasure mystery, however, remains that of Oak Island. The mystery began in 1795, when a teenager named Daniel McGinnis discovered a strange, saucer-shaped depression in a clearing on the wooded island. Nearby was a lone oak tree with a ship's tackle hanging from a partly sawed-off limb. McGinnis reasoned that the tackle might have been used to haul something heavy from a hole—perhaps heavy wooden chests that held pirate loot!

McGinnis returned with friends a few days later and began to dig. But all they found was a deep pit with walls of smooth, hard clay and platforms of rotting logs set at 10-foot (3-meter) intervals. Since that time, more than fifteen treasure-hunting expeditions have burrowed deep into the ground trying to find the secret of what has become known as the Money Pit. (As a young man, President Franklin Roosevelt took part in one of the digs.)

All these efforts have so far yielded only a few artifacts. These include bits and pieces of gold chain, a copper coin, a heart-shaped rock, and a stone with strange markings that when deciphered read, "Forty feet below, two million pounds are buried."

Also discovered was an elaborate drainage system that consisted of flood tunnels from the main shaft to the ocean. Buried along the beach was a man-made blanket of coconut fiber, grass, and seaweed. The blanket acted like a gigantic sponge, taking in water at high tide and then pouring it into the flood tunnels through a system of crude box drains. In this way, the pirate bank's main shaft was kept flooded.

But where is the pirate treasure? If the Oak Island Money Pit is like pirate banks that reportedly were found in Haiti and Madagascar, here's how it works:

First, the pirates dug the main shaft. Then any pirate who wanted to hide treasure dug a secret side tunnel that sloped out from the main tunnel and up toward the surface of the ground. At a point about 30 feet (9 meters) from the surface, the pirate would hack out a small vault for the booty. Then the flood tunnels were dug, and the main shaft was flooded. To make a "withdrawal" from the bank, the pirate just had to dig down 30 feet at the exact point where the personal vault was located.

Now a group of Canadian and American treasure seekers hopes to solve the mystery once and for all. Having spent several million dollars on earlier digs, they are now constructing the biggest shaft of all. This one will be about 80 feet (25 meters) in diameter and 200 feet (60 meters) deep. Some 50,000 tons of earth will be removed, and the Money Pit's old flood tunnels will be dammed.

It will cost about $10 million to complete this massive undertaking. But the treasure could be worth much more—estimates run from $500 million to several billion dollars! Of course, if the treasure hunters come up empty-handed, they'll be left with a very expensive hole in the ground.

Not everyone is happy about these efforts —or about the many other treasure hunts that have taken place around the world. Some people are concerned about the harm that may be done to the environment and to archeological sites when treasure hunters begin to dig. And some argue that rich finds like that of the *Atocha* should be placed in museums.

But these concerns aren't likely to stop treasure hunters—not while there may be millions in gold and precious gems to be found. As the British writer Joseph Conrad put it, "There's no getting away from a treasure that once fastens on your mind."

HENRY I. KURTZ
Author, *John and Sebastian Cabot*

HOW DO YOU DEW?

Covered from wing to wing with glittering beads, these insects look as if they've just come home from a ball. But the "beads" they are wearing are actually drops of dew, catching and reflecting the first glimmering light of dawn.

If you get up early in the morning, you have probably seen dew on the leaves and grass. These tiny droplets of water are formed by moisture that's in the air. During the day, as the sun warms the Earth's surface, the moisture is carried in the air in the form of water vapor. But after the sun goes down, the leaves, grass, and other objects on the Earth's surface begin to cool. And as they lose their heat, the air that comes in contact with them is also cooled.

Eventually, the temperature of this air becomes cool enough to allow the water vapor to condense, or change to liquid. (The temperature at which condensation takes place, called the dew point, varies with the amount of moisture in the air.) It is at this point that tiny drops of dew begin to collect.

Dew is most likely to form on clear, calm nights. The Earth's surface cools down less easily on cloudy nights because a cover of clouds acts somewhat like a blanket, holding heat close to the Earth. And when wind is constantly circulating the air, the air doesn't stay next to cool objects long enough to reach the dew point.

Dew is also more likely to form on objects that cool quickly. Often this is because these objects are very small or thin, as leaves and grasses—and insects—are. Insects are cold-blooded and depend on the sun for warmth. At night, they lose heat.

Some insects are drenched by droplets whenever dew forms—even every night. Butterflies (such as the European skipper on the opposite page, left) and dragonflies (opposite page, top) spend their day on the wing. At night, they simply find a convenient perch on which to rest. Bees and many other insects live in colonies, and they usually return to their hives or nests for the night. But sometimes, for whatever reason, an insect like the bumblebee above will spend a night outside—and end up sleeping under a blanket of dew.

The first rays of the sun turn these dew-soaked insects into glittering, fairylike creatures. They crawl upward to the tips of their branches to capture the warmth. And gradually, the tiny droplets of dew evaporate in the sunlight. Then, their wings finally dry, the insects fly off to begin a new day.

Is this a picture of the future? Scientists think that much of the world will experience oppressive heat if a warming trend called the greenhouse effect continues.

LIFE IN A GREENHOUSE

August, 2040: Washington, D.C., has been broiling in temperatures of over 100°F (38°C) for a week. The news from the Midwest is grim—it looks like another year of poor crops as heat and drought continue to bake the once-fertile plains into a near desert.

California is suffering from a drought, too, and brush fires are raging in the hills. But along the Gulf Coast, the worry is too much water. Rising seas have flooded once-inhabited places in the past few years. Now people are evacuating low-lying areas as a hurricane with winds of up to 160 miles (257 kilometers) an hour approaches.

The situation is even worse in other parts of the world. South Asia is coping with record monsoon rains and a massive refugee problem—in countries such as Bangladesh and the Maldives, so much land has been lost to flooding that millions of people are homeless. In Egypt, large portions of the fertile Nile Delta are now permanently under water, limiting the country's ability to grow food.

This is a view of the world as it might be in 50 years—heat, drought, flooding, food shortages. And the unpleasant predictions have a common source: the greenhouse effect, a worldwide warming trend that many scientists have been forecasting for years. In the 1980's, researchers found strong evidence that this global warming had begun.

A BUILDUP OF GASES

The greenhouse effect is caused by a buildup of carbon dioxide and certain other gases in the Earth's atmosphere. These gases trap heat in much the same way that the glass of a greenhouse does: The gases allow sunlight to pass through the air and warm the Earth, but they don't allow the heat to escape back into space.

Some carbon dioxide has long been present in the atmosphere. In fact, the atmosphere's ability to trap heat probably allowed life to develop on Earth—if some of the sun's warmth weren't retained, the planet would be cold and lifeless.

For at least the past 100,000 years, carbon dioxide levels were relatively stable. Carbon dioxide is produced by animals—you release some every time you exhale. It's also released when living things decay. But it is absorbed by plants, which use it to make food. Thus, living things have helped to keep carbon dioxide in balance.

Now carbon dioxide levels are increasing—because of people. Carbon dioxide is produced when fossil fuels such as coal, oil, and gasoline are burned in homes, cars, factories, and power plants. As the world's population has increased, so has the use of fossil fuels—and so has the output of carbon dioxide. And the carbon dioxide has accumulated in the atmosphere, forming a kind of "blanket" around the Earth.

Other gases that contribute to the greenhouse effect—methane, nitrous oxide, chlorofluorocarbons (CFC's)—are also being released in greater amounts by industry and agriculture. And meanwhile, vast areas of forests have been cleared to make room for farms and towns—destroying trees that otherwise would help absorb carbon dioxide. In many areas, forests have been burned away, producing even more greenhouse gases.

Thus the levels of greenhouse gases have risen steadily since the start of the Industrial Revolution in the mid-1700's. And many people see a direct relation between this change in the atmosphere and a rise in the average annual temperature worldwide. Average temperatures can vary widely from year to year and from place to place, depending on weather patterns. But for more than a century, average temperatures have been rising. In 1988, the worldwide average was higher than any year on record. Scientists later traced the record high to shifts in natural weather patterns, but this didn't change the view that the greenhouse effect might be responsible for the gradual long-term warming of the world.

If this warming trend continues—as many scientists think it will—the result will be an increase of three to nine degrees in the average annual temperature by the middle of the next century. That may not sound like much, but it would roughly equal the amount that the Earth has warmed in the last 10,000 years. And the effects could be devastating.

A HOTTER, WETTER WORLD

Using computer projections, scientists have worked out several possible results of the greenhouse effect. One of the most serious would be melting of the polar ice caps. This would raise sea levels, putting many low-lying areas under water and placing others at risk of flooding in storms. Thousands of homes, farms, and even some towns could be lost to the rising seas. Coastal wetlands would also be destroyed—and along with them, many animal species.

It seems likely, too, that the temperature increase would be uneven: Temperatures around the equator would increase less than those in higher latitudes, where the average might rise as much as twenty degrees. As weather patterns shifted, some areas might even become cooler for a while.

Along with rising temperatures would come an overall increase in precipitation. But this, too, would be uneven. Some areas, such as India and East Africa, might receive much more rain. Others, such as the central plains of North America, would become much drier. Meanwhile, the heat would cause inland lakes to evaporate more quickly, lowering water levels. Chicago might be surrounded by mudflats as Lake Michigan receded.

Warmer temperatures would have still other effects on the weather. Hurricanes and similar tropical storms, for example, feed on warm air. Thus these storms might be more frequent and more destructive in the future.

It's possible that some areas would benefit from the changes. Northern countries such as Canada and the Soviet Union might have longer growing seasons. And higher levels of carbon dioxide could help plants grow, increasing crop yields.

But for the most part, scientists think, the greenhouse effect would be harmful. The Earth's climate has gone through many major changes in the past. But these changes always took place over thousands of years. Plants and animals had time to adjust to the new conditions as they developed. But the current changes are taking place far more rapidly.

If, over the next fifty years or so, heat and drought cause forests to die out in one area, there won't be time for new forests to develop. Animals may not have time to find new sources of food as old ones are destroyed. And the greenhouse effect could create enormous social and political problems, as people compete for scarcer food and water.

Predicting the precise results of the greenhouse effect is extremely difficult. Weather patterns are so complicated that forecasters find it hard to make accurate predictions for a few weeks in the future, let alone years. And it's still not clear how Earth will react to the warming trend.

Natural forces may even help slow the greenhouse effect. For example, heat is absorbed by the ocean. So is carbon dioxide—it is taken in by millions of tiny one-celled plants that live in the sea. But no one knows how much warmth or carbon dioxide the ocean can absorb. It is also possible that, as the world becomes warmer and wetter, cloudy skies will block the sun and help cool the Earth. But no one knows for sure. And scientists say that too much is at stake to simply wait and see.

The greenhouse effect is caused by high levels of carbon dioxide and other gases in the atmosphere. The gases trap the sun's heat and prevent it from escaping back into space, thus causing temperatures to rise.

TAKING ACTION

Can the greenhouse effect be stopped? Halting the buildup of greenhouse gases would be a tall order. By some estimates, worldwide use of fossil fuels would have to be cut by 60 percent. That would mean drastic changes in the way people live—in transportation, industry, agriculture, and countless other aspects of life.

It's unlikely that fuel use will be cut by this much. In fact, some experts predict that the use of fossil fuels will grow in years to come, as undeveloped nations catch up to industrial countries. The warming trend itself might increase fossil fuel usage—air conditioning uses electricity, and most electricity is produced in power plants that burn coal or oil.

Serious conservation efforts could make a difference, however. People in the United States are particularly wasteful when it comes to energy; they use about twice as much as people in Europe and Japan.

Besides using less energy, people could use energy sources that produce less carbon dioxide (such as natural gas) or no carbon dioxide (such as solar and nuclear energy). And they could work hard to preserve forests, which help draw carbon dioxide from the air.

Conservation measures such as these would slow the greenhouse effect and buy valuable time. If the global warming doesn't take place too quickly, researchers may be able to develop crops that are more resistant to heat and drought. Sea walls might be built to protect coastal cities such as New York and Boston. People who live in areas that can't be protected would have more time to relocate.

Some scientists have proposed even stronger steps: planting new forests, creating artificial clouds by dumping sulfur dioxide into the atmosphere to block the sun's rays, or fertilizing the oceans to increase the growth of the one-celled plants that absorb carbon dioxide. CFC's might be blasted out of the atmosphere with laser beams. Huge orbiting parasols might help shade the Earth.

There are problems with most of these plans. New forests would have to cover an area four-and-a-half times the size of California to reduce carbon dioxide levels by a third. Sulfur dioxide causes acid rain, which is harmful to the environment. Powerful laser beams would use huge amounts of energy—and so add to the greenhouse problem. Orbiting parasols would need a total surface area larger than that of the entire United States to have any significant effect.

For the time being, conservation seems to be the most likely way to curb the greenhouse effect. But conservation measures will have to be taken worldwide. A few steps have already been taken. In 1987, many nations agreed to gradually reduce their production of CFC's. In 1989, they met to work out a shorter timetable for phasing out these substances. And representatives of seventeen countries formed a group to study the greenhouse problem. They were to present their proposals to an international conference in 1990. The goal of the conference would be a treaty outlining united action against the greenhouse effect.

INDEX

ILLUSTRATION CREDITS AND ACKNOWLEDGMENTS

14 © James L. Castner
15 © John E. Swedberg—Bruce Coleman Inc.
16 © 1985 K. G. Preston-Marfhan—Discover Publications
17 © 1985 K. G. Preston-Marfhan—Discover Publications; © James L. Castner
18 © Jane Burton—Bruce Coleman Inc.
19 © G. I. Bernard/Oxford Scientific Films—Animals Animals
20 © E. R. Degginger—Bruce Coleman Inc.
21 © Zig Leszczynski—Animals Animals
22 *Creatures of the Desert World,* © 1987 National Geographic Society; *Hot Pursuit,* by Kees Moerbeek and Carla Dijs, © 1987 by Intervisual Communications, Inc. Published by Price/Stern/Sloan Inc.; *The Land of Long Ago—A Visit to Fairyland with Humpty Dumpty,* property of Intervisual Communications Inc.
23 *Lavinia's Cottage,* © 1982 by John S. Goodall. A Margaret K. McElderry Book, Atheneum, 1983, New York; Art Resource/Cooper Hewitt Museum, © 1935; *The Human Body,* by Jonathan Miller, © 1983 by Dark Horse Productions Limited. Published by Viking Penguin Inc., New York
24–26 © John Huehnergarth
29 Courtesy, CBS; Photofest
30 Photofest
31 Photofest; Howard Frank Archives
32 Howard Frank Archives; © Children's Television Workshop
33 Merv Griffin Enterprises; Courtesy, NBC
38 © Dwight R. Kuhn; © Rod Plank—Tom Stack & Associates
39 © Stephen J. Krasemann—DRK Photos; © Dwight R. Kuhn
40–43 Illustrations from *The New Dinosaurs: An Alternative Evolution,* by Dougal Dixon. Copyright © Eddison Sadd Editions 1988. Published by Salem House/Harper & Row, New York, 1988 (hardback) and Ballantine Books, New York, 1989 (paperback). Artist: Steve Holden (Cutlasstooth and Lank), Amanda Barlow (Kloon), Sean Milne (Sift), Martin Knowelden (Crackbeak), Denys Oyenden (Dwarf Megalosaur), and Philip Hood (Sandle and Mountain Leaper)
46 © Tom Ives
49 The Granger Collection
50 © 1989 Children's Television Workshop. Courtesy, *Sesame Street* magazine; © 1985 Erika Stone; UPI—Bettmann Newsphotos
51 © 1988 Michael Greco—Picture Group; © Joe Munroe—Photo Researchers, Inc.
52 © Richard Hutchings—Photo Researchers, Inc.; © 1989 Nick Koudis
53 © Al Freni—*Life* magazine, © 1979 Time Inc.
60–62 © Kjell B. Sandved
63 © Ken W. Davis—Tom Stack & Associates
64–67 © David Macdonald—Animals Animals
68–69 © R. Maiman—Sygma
70 © Sonia Sheridan—Photo Researchers, Inc.
71 © 1989 Barbara Joffe
72–73 © 1987 Pixar
75 Artist, Sharon Holme
76 © Joseph MacNally—Sygma
77 © 1989 The Walt Disney Company
78 © Henson Associates, Inc.
79 © 1989 The Walt Disney Company
80 © John McDermott—Sipa Press
81 Tree designed and created by Jenny Tesar
86–89 Courtesy, Scholastic Photography Awards, conducted by Scholastic Magazines Inc.
90–91 D. Serrette, collections MNHN de Paris
92 D. Serrette, © 1981 Discover Publications
94–95 © Wayne Source
96 Courtesy, NASA
97 Created by Jenny Tesar
98 © Thomas S. England
99 © Gerry Ellis—Ellis Wildlife
101 © Ron Austing—Photo Researchers, Inc.
102 © Ron Garrison—Zoological Society of San Diego
103 Zoological Society of San Diego
113 © Don Kincaid
114 Artist, Sharon Holme
116 © Larry West; © John Shaw
117 © Larry West
118 © Craig Aurness—West Light
120 Artist, Frank Senyk